DEAD WRONG 2:

DIANA, PRINCESS OF WALES

Ri…

David Wayne…

Dead Wrong 2: Diana, Princess of Wales

Cover art and design by Marija Vilotijevic

Published by Vigliano Books
http://www.viglianoassociates.com

Printed in the United States of America.

At White House with John Travolta

Diana's body was immediately embalmed—even though that was illegal—which then made it impossible to determine if she was pregnant. Police tried to get the jeweler who sold Dodi the engagement ring earlier that evening to lie and say that it was not for their engagement. He refused. (Photo courtesy of Ronald Reagan Library)

Diana specifically predicted that she would be assassinated. She wrote that “my husband is planning ‘an accident’ in my car” and “the brakes of my car have been tampered with. If something does happen to me it will be MI5 or MI6 who will have done it.” She also knew she was under electronic surveillance by British Intelligence.

As the car pulls away from the rear of the Paris Ritz, Diana looks back at the press being left behind, Dodi Al-Fayed sits calmly, bodyguard Trevor Rees-Jones assesses the forward path, and driver Henri Paul makes a rapid exit. Stories that the driver was drunk were fabricated; he was not. Also contrary to the official explanation, Diana's car was not closely followed by photographers and that was not the cause of the crash. (Rex USA)

The Mercedes was diverted into the tunnel by vehicles that blocked its exit. The tunnel wasn't the planned route to their destination, which was Dodi's Paris apartment. Then, once inside the tunnel, other vehicles intentionally interfered with the Mercedes, blocking it in and causing it to crash. The Mercedes had recently been stolen and had its computer chip changed out. The laser-like flash of light, and the explosion and blackout of the car's lights before the crash, are highly suggestive of an assassination technique known as "The Boston Brakes" that hijacks the car's computerized systems.

Note the extremely narrow ledge on the left of the roadway where a solid eyewitness noted that he saw a dozen suspicious men standing precariously and observing the crash as it occurred. They quickly vanished after the accident. Diana always wore her seat belt, but hers was defective on the night of the crash. And in yet another odd "coincidence," the regular traffic cameras in the tunnel were not functioning at the time of the crash, so there was no recording of it as there would normally be. (Rex USA)

First physician on the scene, Dr. Mailliez, administering to Diana, who is in the right rear seat. Note the limited damage to the vehicle. Damage increased later as a result of prying open the car to access the victims on the driver side. To the first doctor's astonishment—even though she was not pinned in the vehicle and clearly exhibited the external signs of internal bleeding— it took emergency crews an incredibly long 1 hour, 40 minutes to get Diana to a nearby hospital; and she bled to death as a result. (Rex USA)

(Chart courtesy of *Daily Mail UK*, August 30, 2013, in Sue Reid: "Diana, that SAS murder claim")

DEAD WRONG 2:

DIANA, PRINCESS OF WALES

To understand a person's death, it's a good idea to first understand what was going on in their life.

We all know the formal picture that's been painted of Diana Spencer, Princess of Wales.

Lady Diana was the first wife of Prince Charles, heir apparent to Queen Elizabeth II. Their royal wedding in 1981 was a global event, viewed on television by close to a billion people. Her marriage to the Prince of Wales—which bore two children who are currently in the line of succession to the British throne—ended in divorce in 1996. She then died in a horrific car crash in a Paris tunnel in 1997.

And we all tend to look at Lady Diana in that larger-than-life manner. But is it accurate?

In a word: No.

So first, let's take an intimate look at the real woman whom Diana Spencer had become.

On one occasion, she reportedly went out on a date with a man she admired *wearing nothing but a fur coat.*[1]

---

[1] Paul Burrell, *A Royal Duty* (Putnam: 2003); James Mills & Andy Dolan, "Diana 'wanted to wed doctor'," *Daily* Mail, retrieved 26 August 2013: http://www.dailymail.co.uk/news/article-146022/Diana-wanted-wed-doctor.html

Have we got your attention now? *Good.* So if you hadn't known that before, then you better keep reading.

Here it is, in a nutshell: short, with both the sweet and the bittersweet.

She separated from Prince Charles in 1992. That made her an outcast in the Royal Family, but her popularity with the public actually grew—they were quite attached to her charismatic charms. So the fact that she had obviously been ostracized by the Royal Family yet was much more popular than they were made her, to them, something of a royal pain in the neck—maybe lower.

Instead of just going off somewhere to disappear, as was apparently proper and expected, Diana reinvented herself. She went around the world, hugging the victims of British land mines. Her warmth was genuine and contagious and no one felt it brighter and truer than those who were lucky enough to be in her path.

But the Brits back home felt her magic also. And that made her even more unpopular with the "Royals"; she wouldn't go quietly and they didn't quite know what to do about her. Though shunned officially, she remained in the public eye, raising her two young children as she saw fit in a manner that was probably not in proper British form, at least insofar as the Queen was concerned—and you've gotta like that! She also had a string of very public affairs and that infuriated the Royals even more. Having been the "black sheep" of the Royal Family since her entry, her exit certainly left a wake of British expletives scattered around the palace—and we're talking about words even harsher than the notorious *Bloody hell.*

Suffice to say that she remained a world famous celebrity and used that popularity for a higher purpose; to raise funds and promote charitable causes, primarily related to children and health. While much of the Royal Family was all aflutter with the usual priorities of the ruling class—like what to wear to the next polo match—Diana was directing her attention to things that actually mattered, like helping the 99.999 percent of the planet who hadn't been born into a family where mismatched argyle socks were considered a national tragedy of the utmost historical significance. As I candidly pointed out years ago on my show called *The Belzer Connection*, these people have been marrying their own cousins for eleven hundred years—it's a miracle they can floss their own teeth. To say that Diana was a breath of fresh air is like saying it was kind of nice when the Spanish Inquisition was over—it was called the Dark Ages for a reason, folks.

After "Lady Di"—the name by which she was revered by her loving public— discarded the posh trappings of the Royal Family, she quite clearly became "her own person," as the old expression goes. And that person was actually quite an interesting individual—a point which might surprise you if you've seen a picture of the Queen of England at any time during the last twenty years—but we digress.

"Ever since the separation in 1992, she felt she had grown in stature, and she was ready to take on the world in her humanitarian mission. But, rightly or wrongly, she felt the stronger she became, the more she was regarded as a modernizing nuisance who was prepared to go out on a limb and do the unconventional.

She was later to be proved right, to some degree, when her humanitarian work in Angola in early 1997 led to suggestions that she was a 'loose cannon' who was doing more harm than good."[2]

Diana's personal butler and confidante said that "she had an overpowering feeling she was 'in the way'."[3]

She was also very human. Her loving public dubbed her the "Queen of Hearts" for a very good reason—because they could tell that she actually had one.

While estranged from her husband, in 1995, Diana met a handsome Pakistani surgeon named Hasnat Khan. It was just a chance meeting in an elevator, but Diana described him to a friend with a telling comment: "Drop-dead gorgeous."

Dr. Khan is a man of immense integrity who genuinely cared about Diana as a person, and he has shunned the limelight in this case, avoiding publicity or the temptation of "selling" his story. He's been too busy doing things that actually matter, like building hospitals to help the children who suffer from the "collateral damage" of the wars being waged around the world. It would appear, therefore, that we can trust his account.

He met Diana again when she came to visit a friend of hers who was in the hospital. They became friendly on her subsequent visits to see her friend. One day, they had been chatting, and Dr. Khan mentioned that he had to pick up some books at his uncle's house in the English countryside. Never thinking she would

---

[2] Burrell, *A Royal Duty*
[3] Ibid.

accept—he knew she was the Princess of Wales—he asked her if she'd like to come.[4]

Much to his surprise, she accepted the offer. They took that drive, visited with his aunt and uncle out in the country, then went out to dinner later that night. Their friendship quickly developed into a romantic relationship.[5]

In fact, their relationship became so serious that Diana was actually considering moving to Pakistan and converting her faith to Islam.[6] She even asked her private butler to investigate the possibility of securing a priest to perform a secret marriage.[7]

As their relationship was approaching two years together—with Lady Di sneaking around London in long dark wigs to go unspotted during their many secret rendezvous—Dr. Khan realized the hard reality and told Diana. The relationship wasn't capable of progressing due to a number of stumbling blocks. It wasn't just that they were from different cultures and different religions. Diana, as an international megastar, was constantly in the spotlight and that constant media

---

4 *The Associated Press*, "Ex-boyfriend doubted Princess Diana pregnancy," March 3, 2008: http://usatoday30.usatoday.com/news/world/2008-03-03-diana-inquest_N.htm

5 Ibid.

6 *The Telegraph*, "Dr Hasnat Khan: the heart surgeon who Princess Diana dubbed Mr Wonderful," November 7, 2011: http://www.telegraph.co.uk/news/newstopics/diana/8874787/Dr-Hasnat-Khan-the-heart-surgeon-who-Princess-Diana-dubbed-Mr-Wonderful.html

7 Ibid.

hyper-scrutiny precluded the possibility of having any semblance of a normal life together.[8]

Ultimately, as Dr. Khan explained it, there was no way the relationship could really work. If they married, then to have anything close to a normal life together, they would have to live in Pakistan. Realistically, she couldn't live in Pakistan. And the Royal Family would never allow that for her two young children because of the fact they are heirs to the British throne. So he felt overwhelmed by the impossibility of the relationship progressing.[9]

So they broke off the affair and it wasn't a happy ending. In fact, Diana's friends reiterated on many occasions that she'd told them Dr. Khan was "the love of her life" and that, even after their split, everything that she did was geared toward creating jealousy in Khan.[10] When she was photographed in public with another man—it was because she hoped it would make him jealous. When she let herself be photographed in a

---

[8] Andrew Morton, "Diana, Princess of Wales: The affair of the heart that was her final obsession," August 3, 2013, *The Telegraph*: http://www.telegraph.co.uk/news/newstopics/diana/10220421/Diana-Princess-of-Wales-The-affair-of-the-heart-that-was-her-final-obsession.html

[9] Ibid.

[10] Sarah Ellison, "The Mystery Man Who Stole the Princess's Heart," September 2013, *Vanity Fair*: http://www.usmagazine.com/celebrity-news/news/princess-diana-wanted-to-marry-hasnat-khan-was-madly-in-love-2013307; Morton, "Diana, Princess of Wales: The affair of the heart that was her final obsession"; Massoud Ansari & Andrew Alderson, "Dr Hasnat Khan: Princess Diana and me," January 13, 2008: http://www.telegraph.co.uk/news/uknews/1575413/Dr-Hasnat-Khan-Princess-Diana-and-me.html

sexy bikini at the beach—it was because she hoped Khan would see it.[11]

Then Diana met Dodi.

But *first*, like any family in British society—and most especially, the *Royal* Family itself—we, of course, need to pay heed to the words of the one person who actually knew what the hell was going on with everyone... The Butler! If you hadn't realized that, you've obviously never lived in proper British society—*and* have not watched television for a couple of decades—here, here!

Quaint as the custom may seem, Diana had a personal butler who actually *did* know most of what was going on—and, having been there, we expected nothing less.

THE BUTLER ALWAYS KNOWS

The British court system was certainly keen on that point. When *they* wanted to learn what the hell was actually happening in the Royal Family they immediately figured out exactly how to go about finding that out: You *ask the butler*.

His name is Paul Burrell and he actually *was* called by the British authorities to provide testimony. We know from testimony that:

---

[11] Morton, "Diana, Princess of Wales: The affair of the heart that was her final obsession"

Diana was an independent woman—in fact, confident enough to leave the house, completely naked under a fur coat, for a rendezvous with her lover;

Diana was a woman who enjoyed the romantic intimacy of a relationship with a man;

She used contraception regularly, or at least we know that she did during the period of her two-year relationship with Dr. Khan;[12]

She was very much in love with the good doctor. She described the man of her dreams as "Mr. Wonderful" and "The One"; friends said she made it clear that he was "the love of her life." It was obviously a very serious relationship, on both sides.[13] Sadly, the relationship ended because the obstacles to its progressing appeared insurmountable.

And what, dare one ask, did Diana's mother do? She called her "a whore" for "fucking around with Muslim men."[14] Great, huh? I bet that was fun to listen to. And the butler actually did listen in on that phone call. Diana shared all her exploits with him—and you've gotta like that!

---

[12] "Dr Hasnat Khan: the heart surgeon who Princess Diana dubbed Mr Wonderful," The Telegraph, 11-07-2011; "Diana, Princess of Wales: The affair of the heart that was her final obsession," Andrew Morton, 11-03-2013.

[13] "Diana 'wanted to wed doctor'," James Mills & Andy Dolan, Daily Mail; "Ex-boyfriend doubted Princess Diana pregnancy," AP, 3-03-2008

[14] Robert Barr, "Princess Diana's secret safe with loyal butler," January 15, 2008: http://usatoday30.usatoday.com/life/people/2008-01-14-diana_N.htm

That same butler also told authorities that another member of the Royal Family had told Diana that she should beware that she was under surveillance.[15]

And get a load of this little gem that comes to us direct from the Queen of England: Queen Elizabeth II (*yes, THE* Queen) had a conversation with that same butler, in which she warned him to be careful. She said:

"There are powers at work in this country of which we have no knowledge."[16]

Enter Dodi Fayed: The rich, handsome son of Egyptian multibillionaire, Mohamed Al-Fayed. He had a bit of a "playboy" reputation—as the younger set would say, a *player.*

He "courts" Diana and the two, very quickly, become very serious. In the weeks before her death, Diana spends more time with Dodi and his father on their yacht than she does anywhere else.

Diana accompanies Dodi back to Paris and they go to the luxurious Ritz Hotel, root of the word "ritzy." They always have a nice room there too because the Fayeds freaking *own the place.*

According to Mohamed Al-Fayed, his son Dodi called him right before the crash and told him that he and Diana were planning to announce their engagement that weekend. Mohamed advised his son to stay put because the press would be all over the story. Dodi answered that they were just going from the Ritz to his

---

[15] Jane Kerr, "Royal Warned Di – 'You Are Being Spied On'," 10-21-2003, *Daily Mirror*: http://rense.com/general43/spied.htm
[16] Barr, "Princess Diana's secret safe with loyal butler"

Paris apartment and would stay there. That journey was fatal for Diana, Dodi and Henri Paul, the driver, head of security at the Ritz for the Fayed family.

We've been around this block a time or two and we've learned that there's a proper way to investigate British history, and then there's a *right* way. So, we did the only thing one can do to learn the truth about the Royal Family. You guessed it. We went back to the butler!

Paul Burrell was a lot more than Diana's right-hand man. He was her friend and safe refuge—one of the very few people in the world whom she knew—beyond the slightest doubt—that she could always trust without hesitation. What the world called her "butler," Diana called safe harbor in any storm.

Mr. Burrell lays out the landscape like this:

"The princess had just finished a long-term relationship with someone she cared deeply about. I know that, because I was there. I saw it."[17]

Mr. Burrell described Diana as being "on the rebound from that relationship when she met someone who was very kind and attentive and generous."[18]

He said the affair with Dr. Khan had lasted at least eighteen months and was dead serious with talk of marriage, children; the whole nine yards. But he described the romance with Fayed as a "30-day

---

[17] Burrell, *A Royal Duty*; Barr, "Princess Diana's secret safe with loyal butler"
[18] Ibid.

relationship."[19] So that's not to say that marriage wasn't possible. In fact, people on the "rebound" often get married very quickly. And, as we've seen, Diana was extremely anxious over the failure of her desperately serious love affair with Dr. Khan.

So Diana was at a very volatile stage. Was a lightning-quick marriage to a brand new boyfriend that would startle the world a realistic possibility at that point?

You can *bet the ranch* it was. In fact, it was more than possible—it was even understandable.

So, now that we've had a true glimpse of the real Diana Spencer, let's take a close look at the actual circumstances of her death.

THE EVIDENCE

Our investigation uncovered some amazing facts. A highly noteworthy point in this case is that the most important facts surrounding the car crash that killed Lady Diana have *not* been emphasized in the media and remain unknown to most people.

1. Diana Correctly Predicted Her Own Murder

Get a load of this!

---

[19] Ibid.

News Flash just in-----

-----Information extremely pertinent to her death.

For openers, any time that you see a credible person going on-the-record that they believe someone may murder them—and they are then murdered in *precisely the manner* they had feared—you have to look at that as an extremely important prediction. That was the case in the death of Dr. David Kelly, as we pointed out in our first book, *Dead Wrong*.

Diana Spencer made a claim—*in writing*—that she feared her murder at the hands of her husband, and even predicted—also in writing—that it would be perpetrated by having something done to her car.

Diana wrote a letter, for protection, in which she specifically predicted that she would be killed via an arranged car accident. She entrusted the letter to her friend, butler Paul Burrell.

Did you hear about that before? Neither did I. You know why? Because the media basically buried it.

But it's true. Diana actually—*on more than one occasion*—specifically alleged that her husband was going to try to kill her *and* that it would be made to look like a car accident!

Isn't that *hugely* relative to a car crash investigation?

So what did everyone do, you might logically ask, such as the authorities and would-be investigative journalists? They *buried it*, of course. It went straight to the bottom of page C47, if it went to press at all. Even many years later, it is still difficult to find a copy of that letter.

To which we say: *Disgraceful!* That's a *huge* piece of evidence. The world has every right and every *need* to know that! That's why she freaking wrote it to begin with! For *protection*! She predicted what would happen *and it did!*

HANDWRITTEN PREDICTION OF MURDER BY HER "ENEMIES"

The following is *a verbatim copy* of a handwritten letter of Lady Diana, written on her own stationery, October 1996 (10 months before her death). Diana entrusted this letter to butler, Paul Burrell, and instructed him to keep it as "insurance" for the future.[20] That's not to be taken lightly. Her exact words follow:

I am sitting here at my desk today in October, longing for someone to hug me & encourage me to keep strong & hold my head high—this particular phase in my life is the most dangerous—my husband is planning "an accident" in my car. Brake failure & serious head injury in order to make the path clear for him to marry Tiggy. Camilla is nothing but a decoy, so we are all being used by the man in every sense of the word.

I have been battered, bruised and abused mentally by a system for 15 years now, but I feel no resentment, I carry no hatred. I am weary of the battles, but I will never surrender. I am strong inside and maybe that is a problem for my enemies.

---

[20] Paul Burrell, *A Royal Duty*, 2003

Thank you Charles, for putting me through such hell and for giving me the opportunity to learn from the cruel things you have done to me. I have gone forward fast and have cried more than anyone will ever know. The anguish nearly killed me, but my inner strength has never let me down, and my guides have taken such good care of me up there. Aren't I fortunate to have had their wings to protect me.[21]

Diana placed the above letter in an envelope and wrote "Paul" on the front of the envelope. Before sealing the envelope, Diana told Paul Burrell:

"I am going to date this and I want you to keep it…just in case."[22]

Diana followed up on those concerns, making the same specific allegation in a meeting—which has been documented—with three of her barristers (attorneys).

In October 1995, Diana met secretly with the highly esteemed Lord Mishcon, Barrister Maggie Rae and Barrister Sandra Ray, a senior partner at the law firm of which Lord Mishcon headed up.[23]

At that meeting, Diana detailed a list of allegations that totally shocked her listeners with an exquisitely specific

---

[21] *Letters of Note,* "My husband is planning 'an accident'," 10-20-2009: http://www.lettersofnote.com/2009/10/my-husband-is-planning-accident-in-my.html

[22] *London Mirror*, "DIANA LETTER SENSATION: 'THEY WILL TRY TO KILL ME'," 10-11-2001: http://thetruthproject.wordpress.com/2001/09/page3/

[23] Gordon Rayner, "Diana warned of 'car crash plot to kill her'," 11-14-2008, *The Telegraph:* http://www.telegraph.co.uk/news/uknews/1575606/Diana-warned-of-car-crash-plot-to-kill-her.html

list of a conspiracy that was in progress in Britain at that time, that she was dead set against. Diana told them that:

- The Queen was planning to abdicate the throne so that Charles would become King of England. Lord Mishcon's notes of that meeting read: "Her Royal Highness" told me that "the Queen would be abdicating in April and the Prince of Wales would then assume the throne."[24]
- "Reliable sources" had informed her of a plan in place to have her *and* Camilla Parker Bowles (Charles' adulteress for many years) "put aside" in order to allow the Prince and soon-to-be King to marry the children's nanny, Tiggy Legge-Bourke.[25]
- "Authorities" were planning to "get rid of her" and make it look like a car accident.[26]
- Lord Mishcon did not mince his words; there was no doubt about it. His further notes of the meeting read: Her Royal Highness "was convinced that there was a conspiracy that she and Camilla would be put aside."[27]
- Diana also told the three lawyers that the children's nanny had undergone an abortion and that she was in the process of obtaining medical documentation that would prove it.[28]

---

[24] Rebecca English & Michael Seamark, "Diana told top lawyer Queen was about to abdicate…and she feared for her life," 10-03-2007, *Daily Mail*: http://www.dailymail.co.uk/news/article-485314/Diana-told-lawyer-Queen-abdicate---feared-life.html
[25] Ibid.
[26] Ibid.
[27] Ibid.
[28] Ibid.

A ROYAL CONSPIRACY

Lord Mishcon was so distressed about the revelations from his meeting with Princess Diana that he saw fit to document them for the record. The following are his exact notes from that meeting:

"Her Royal Highness said that she had been informed by reliable sources, whom she did not want to reveal, as they would very quickly dry up if she did, that:

A. The Queen would be abdicating in April and the Prince of Wales would then be assuming the throne, and
B. Efforts would then be made, if not to get rid of her, be it by some accident in her car, such as prepared brake failure or whatever, between now and then, at least to see that she was so injured or damaged as to be declared 'unbalanced.'

"She was convinced that there was a conspiracy and that she and Camilla Parker Bowles were to be put aside.

She had also been told that Miss Legge Bourke had been operated on for an abortion and that she, HRH, would soon be in receipt of 'a certificate'.

I told HRH that if she really believed her life was being threatened, security measures, including those on her car, must be increased.

HRH said that in her view the best solution for the future of the monarchy was for the Prince of Wales to abdicate in favour of Prince William."

Another attorney present at the same meeting, Maggie Rae, concluded that:

"It was very clear in my own mind that she thought she was going to be killed."[29]

Diana also confided in friends that she was facing a very real threat.

DIANA KNEW HER LIFE WAS IN DANGER

Just two months before her death, Diana confided in a biographer with whom she had become friends, Ingrid Seward. The two had a long "girlie chat," as Diana called them, and she really opened up to her friend.
The following quotes are her friend's recollections of that conversation:

"We were having what she called a girlie chat and she just opened up. She told me exactly what she said in her letter to Burrell.

"She told me: 'I know this sounds silly now, but I did really worry about the brakes on my car'. Diana said this to me at the end of June 1997. She was convinced

[29] "Diana warned of 'car crash plot to kill her'," Gordon Rayner, 1-14-2008, *The Telegraph:*
http://www.telegraph.co.uk/news/uknews/1575606/Diana-warned-of-car-crash-plot-to-kill-her.html

there were people out to get her. We laughed about it. She didn't tell me who they were. She was quite canny.

"She obviously took it quite seriously and said that she had the apartment swept for bugs."

"I spent the morning with her. Everything she told me was amazing. I was under trust not to repeat what she said. I couldn't believe what she was saying. It was pretty extraordinary."

"Diana avoided saying who these people were who were after her."

"She was trying to emphasize the mistrust she felt for everybody and feeling completely isolated. It must have been pretty scary."

"I knew she was also fearful they would take the boys away from her, and was genuinely worried that would happen."[30]

An established record exists that is filled with red-flag warnings related to Diana's clear perception that she was going to be murdered.

In 1995, Diana wrote the following in a note to her friend, Simone Simmons:

---

30 "DI TOLD ME SHE WAS IN DANGER," *London Mirror*, 9-11-2001: http://thetruthproject.wordpress.com/2001/09/page/3/

"Dear Simone, as you know, the brakes of my car have been tampered with. If something does happen to me it will be MI5 or MI6 who will have done it. Lots of love, Diana."[31]

The official British investigation contained info that Diana had stated the following in November, 1995:

"Prince Philip wants to see me dead."[32]

In August 1996 Diana told her friend Roberto Devorik:

"I am a threat in their eyes. They only use me when they need me for official functions and then they drop me again in the darkness… they are not going to kill me by poisoning me or in a big plane where others will get hurt. They will either do it when I am on a small plane, in a car when I am driving or in a helicopter."[33]

Diana's close personal involvement in the anti-weapons movement reportedly caused widespread anger among Western governments and the armament industry.

When Diana returned from her peace mission to Angola in 1997—just weeks before her death—she was reportedly warned by a high-ranking personal friend of Prince Charles. Nicolas Soames, a former Defense Minister of Great Britain, was an MP (Member of Parliament, the equivalent to a U.S. congressman). He called Diana and reportedly stated:

---

[31] King & Beveridge, *Princess Diana: The Hidden Evidence*: http://www.whale.to/c/princess_diana9.html
[32] King & Beveridge, *Princess Diana: The Hidden Evidence*, citing "Operation Paget Report," page 108
[33] King & Beveridge, *Princess Diana: The Hidden Evidence*: http://www.whale.to/c/princess_diana9.html

"Don't meddle in things that you know nothing about because you know accidents can happen."[34]

Significantly, it should be noted that "Diana's murder happened just three weeks before the Oslo conference to ban anti-personnel mines. Without Diana as the most prominent ambassador of the conference, most of the world's media no longer bothered to attend."[35]

And in October 2003, Mohamed Al-Fayed, who had spent a great deal of time with Diana in the weeks just prior to her death, stated that:

"Diana told me personally, during a holiday in the South of France, that the person who is spearheading these threats is Prince Philip… She told me it would happen either in a helicopter or a car."[36]

Diana had actually made another allegation in the warning letter she gave to her butler. She specifically predicted that Camilla Parker Bowles would also be murdered, because both Camilla and Diana were on a government hit list.[37] Mrs. Bowles, who had been

---

[34] *Unlawful Killing* (documentary), directed by Keith Allen, 2011: https://www.youtube.com/watch?v=Wf1Gh1VyjqA; King & Beveridge, *Princess Diana: The Hidden Evidence*

[35] *Rebel of Oz*, "The Unlawful Killing of Princess Diana and Dodi Al-Fayed," March 8, 2013: http://beforeitsnews.com/conspiracy-theories/2013/03/the-unlawful-killing-of-princess-diana-and-dodi-al-fayed-2449166.html?currentSplittedPage=2

[36] King & Beveridge, *Princess Diana: The Hidden Evidence*: http://www.whale.to/c/princess_diana9.html

[37] King & Beveridge, *Princess Diana: The Hidden Evidence*: http://www.whale.to/c/princess_diana9.html; Everard & Houston, *Lady Die: The Diana Conspiracies*: http://www.youtube.com/watch?v=Nr54FXg7ASI

having an affair with Diana's husband, Prince Charles for many years, did indeed have an attempt on her life after Diana's letter was written. And "that assassination attempt had taken the form of a road traffic accident."[38] That incident was nearly fatal and took place about six weeks prior to Diana's car accident.

Camilla Parker-Bowles herself acted very oddly in the course of those events. Leaving the scene of accident in Britain is a huge criminal offense—it's practically beaten into everyone that if you're involved in a road accident, it's your utmost legal obligation to wait at the scene until the police arrive. Yet, after the road accident in the car Camilla Parker-Bowles had been driving, it's reported that she not only fled the scene, but ran frantically into the woods, which has led to suggestions that the car crash was an orchestrated murder attempt and that she herself knew that someone was attempting to kill her.[39]

It should be added that Diana also believed that her ex-bodyguard, Barry Mannakee, who was also her lover for a period of time, had been murdered by MI5, the elite British internal security organization.[40] Mr. Manakee was also killed in a road traffic accident. "She was convinced that that was an MI5 operation that killed him."[41]

So Diana clearly believed—and left clear pieces of evidence vividly demonstrating the fact—that if she was

[38] Ibid.
[39] Ibid.
[40] Ibid.
[41] Ibid.

murdered, the blame for ordering her killed rested with the Royal Family.

Mohamed Al-Fayed thought the same thing. And still does.

The extensive investigation of Mohamed Al-Fayed, the father of Dodi whom he swears was secretly engaged to Diana, substantiates those findings. Mr. Al-Fayed, a multibillionaire who used all resources available to determine what happened, is not a man to be taken lightly. To say he is unswerving in his very direct accusation that it is the British Royals and intelligence agencies which are responsible for the mass murder would be dramatic understatement. He is absolutely and positively certain.

So, to fully absorb the tremendous gravity of this point, simply ask yourself this:

If you learned that your next door neighbor had died in a car accident and that people immediately began saying it was suspicious, and you learned that she had written a letter to a friend for "safekeeping" specifically stating that her husband was planning to kill her by causing a car accident—plus she had met with three attorneys and voiced the exact same concerns, which they took seriously enough to document in letters at the time:

Based on that evidence alone—Wouldn't you expect a murder investigation to take place? Well—it didn't. And still hasn't.

2. **Diana Knew That She Was Under Electronic Surveillance**

Every move and word of Lady Diana was being tracked by British Intelligence agencies—and she knew it.

Documented evidence exists that Diana *knew* that her apartment had been bugged with electronic listening devices and also that her phones were all tapped by Her Majesty's intelligence services.[42]

A member of the Royal Family had warned her pointedly:

"You need to be discreet, even in your own home, because 'they' are listening all the time."[43]

Diana was, in fact, so certain that British Intelligence services were bugging her apartment and phone calls, that she would don a disguise and walk to public telephone booths to make her phone calls.[44]

"In the final two years of her life, the princess grew increasingly concerned about the security around her."[45]

Diana's fears reached the extent that she was certain she was under surveillance. She and her butler, Paul,

---

[42] Jon King & John Beveridge, *Princess Diana: The Hidden Evidence* (S.P.I. Books: 2001); *Lady Die: The Diana Conspiracies – An Investigation Into The Killing of HRH Princess Diana* (Dvd), directed by Chris Everard & Raphaella Houston, 2009: http://www.youtube.com/watch?v=KSnaki4WKpw

[43] Burrell, *A Royal Duty;* Kerr, "Royal Warned Di – 'You Are Being Spied On'"

[44] Everard & Houston, *Lady Die: The Diana Conspiracies*: http://www.youtube.com/watch?v=KSnaki4WKpw

[45] Burrell, *A Royal Duty*

turned her residences upside down looking for electronic listening devices but found none. So she had her residences swept for "bugs" by a professional.[46] Her butler tells the story:

"When she found none, she called on the help of her ex-intelligence services friend.

One weekend afternoon he visited the palace using a pseudonym. He carried out a sweep of the apartments to detect listening devices. Every room was checked, nothing was found."[47]

Although none were found, her fears deepened when she learned that technology had made eavesdropping a lot simpler than that. She and her friend Paul were about to get an education in surveillance techniques; he describes how the class came about, right in the Princess's residence, after their "sweep" had revealed no equipment:

"Then, in demonstration after demonstration, the princess and I were given a sharp lesson in high-tech surveillance techniques.

But what startled the princess most was to learn that 'monitoring' did not necessarily require devices to be planted in a household.

So high-tech were the intelligence facilities that a conversation could be listened to from a surveillance

---

[46] Burrell, *A Royal Duty*; *London Mirror*, "DIANA LETTER SENSATION: 'THEY WILL TRY TO KILL ME'," September 11, 2001: http://thetruthproject.wordpress.com/2001/09/page3/
[47] Burrell, *A Royal Duty*

van parked outside, transmitting a signal into the building and using mirrors to bounce it back.

As a result, she took down the round convex mirror that hung above the marble fireplace opposite the window in the sitting room.

She was not paranoid: she was being advised."[48]

It's been proven that Diana's fears were *not* imagined, but very real.

She was indeed under surveillance:

"The fact that these conversations—these private telephone conversations between Diana and Mr. Gilby—came to light in the press, *proves* that Diana was *not* paranoid. She was *not* hallucinating. She wasn't a victim of wild speculation. It *proves* that people *really* were spying on Diana."[49]

3. **Diana Always Wore Her Seatbelt — But the Seatbelt in the Mercedes Had Been Jammed Into a Defective Position**

It has been established that Diana always wore her seatbelt.

---

[48] Ibid.

[49] Everard & Houston, *Lady Die: The Diana Conspiracies*: http://www.youtube.com/watch?v=KSnaki4WKpw

Recall Dr. Khan, who was the Pakistani doctor whom friends of Diana maintained was the true "love of her life":[50]

He stated that he was surprised that Diana had not been strapped in because "she was always very particular about putting her seat belt on."[51]

Yet she was *not* wearing her seatbelt on the night of the fatal crash.

Why not? Because the seatbelt in the right rear seat of the rented Mercedes limousine had somehow been jammed in a defective position. Even the official British investigation confirmed that finding.[52] Wasn't that convenient?

On top of that, that *particular* limo with the unworkable seatbelt—was the only one said to be available that night for the trip from the Paris Ritz Hotel to Dodi's Paris apartment.[53]

TOO BAD TO BE TRUE

It simply exceeds the limits of coincidence that:

---

[50] Ellison, "The Mystery Man Who Stole the Princess's Heart"; Morton, "Diana, Princess of Wales: The affair of the heart that was her final obsession"; Ansari & Alderson, "Dr Hasnat Khan: Princess Diana and me"

[51] *The Associated Press*, "Ex-boyfriend doubted Princess Diana pregnancy": http://usatoday30.usatoday.com/news/world/2008-03-03-diana-inquest_N.htm

[52] King & Beveridge, *Princess Diana: The Hidden Evidence*: http://www.whale.to/c/princess_diana9.html

[53] Ibid.

A. A limousine that was knowingly being furnished to a member of the Royal Family;
B. For a client who insisted upon no less than perfect security precautions;
C. Had a defective seatbelt in precisely the location that the Princess of Wales was to be seated;
D. In the only limousine that was available at that time for service, and therefore;
E. Ensuring that someone who reportedly always wore their seatbelt *was prevented* from doing so;
F. Causing her death under circumstances that were clearly survivable had she been wearing her seatbelt.[54]

The above facts *can* be explained, however, in the context of exactly what transpired with and to that particular limousine in the days immediately prior to the fatal crash.

4. **The Mercedes Limousine Had Recently Been Stolen and Reconfigured**

The Mercedes S280 Sedan that transported Diana on the fatal night had previously been stolen at gunpoint and the engine management microchip had been replaced so that the car could be controlled remotely. It was recovered three days later and the only change noted in it was that it had its EMS (Electronic

---

[54] *Princess Diana: The Hidden Evidence*, Jon King & John Beveridge (S.P.I. Books: 2001): http://www.whale.to/c/princess_diana9.html

Management Systems) chip changed. That chip controlled the car's computerized system, including its steering and brakes.[55]

It's not known who stole the car or who replaced its computer chip. But it *is* known that on the fateful night of Diana's death, her security team was told that the Mercedes S280 was the only car available; the very same one that had been stolen and had a new computer chip put in.[56]

Which all leads us to a well-established sophisticated assassination technique known as "The Boston Brakes."

5. **The Computer-Hacking Assassination Technique: "The Boston Brakes"**

It is now established knowledge that the electronic computer system of a car can be totally taken over—"hacked"— by nefarious outside persons. They can take over the steering, brakes, acceleration—everything.

That news comes to us from no less a source than the highly-esteemed Defense Advanced Research Projects

---

[55] King & Beveridge, *Princess Diana: The Hidden Evidence*; Everard & Houston, *Lady Die: The Diana Conspiracies*: http://www.youtube.com/watch?v=Nr54FXg7ASI

[56] Everard & Houston, *Lady Die: The Diana Conspiracies*: http://www.youtube.com/watch?v=au877N4ryo8; *Princess Diana: The Bizarre Unsolved Disturbing Events Surrounding Her Death*, "Princess Diana's Death: The Mystery of the Stolen Mercedes," 6-29-2007: http://princess-diana-life-n-death.blogspot.com/2007/06/princess-dianas-death-mystery-of-stolen.html

Agency (DARPA), home of the brain-center of technology for the United States government.

Dr. Kathleen Fisher works at DARPA. She's the Program Manager of HACMS: High Assurance Cyber Military Systems and she knows of what she speaks.[57] In a short speech, accessible on the Internet, she lays it all out bare; that, these days, a new, shiny car is really just a big, fat target for the latest software capabilities.[58]

If you want the really short version, here it is, a distilled version of the same speech—a one-minute lesson in "assassination-by-computer software" that will knock your socks right off[59]: http://youtu.be/PNhwEqrtQMk

A car hack can be easily accomplished, DARPA tells us, "taking over all functionality of the car" without even touching the car itself. And DARPA knows because their own researchers actually attempted and accomplished that:

"These attacks involved infecting the computers in the repair shop and then having that infection spread to the car through the diagnostic port. Or hacking in through the Bluetooth system, or using the cellphone network

---

[57] DARPA, "High Assurance Cyber Military Systems (HACMS)," retrieved 9-18-2013: http://www.darpa.mil/Our_Work/I2O/Programs/High-Assurance_Cyber_Military_Systems_%28HACMS%29.aspx

[58] "DARPA PM Kathleen Fisher, High Assurance Systems," retrieved 9-18-2013: http://www.youtube.com/watch?v=3D6jxBDy8k8

[59] "Can a car be hacked? Let's ask DARPA," http://www.youtube.com/watch?v=PNhwEqrtQMk

to break in through the telematics unit that's normally used to provide roadside assistance."[60]

Dr. Fisher revealed that the currently operational methods are much more high-tech than most people are aware:

"The most ingenious attack though used the stereo system in the car. The researchers were able to craft an electronic version of a song that played just fine in your home stereo system or on your personal computer. But when you put that on a CD and played it in the car's CD player, it took over total control of your automobile."[61]

And that's considered "old news" in the high tech department, folks.

We also learned that the same car that was in that high-speed crash had been recently stolen and then recovered and that its electronics system had reportedly been replaced. That fits perfectly with the M.O. for The Boston Brakes.

We actually confirmed several examples of "assassination by traffic accident." It was revealed to investigator Jon King by former SAS (the elite Special Air Services unit) officer, Sir Ranulph Fiennes, that the method had been used by the SAS for assassination and was called "The Boston Brakes," named after the region in northern England where the SAS is based and where they developed the technique:

---

[60] "DARPA PM Kathleen Fisher, High Assurance Systems," retrieved 9-18-2013: http://www.youtube.com/watch?v=3D6jxBDy8k8
[61] Ibid.

"It effectively involves inserting a little microchip transceiver that overrides the steering and the brakes so that the car can be remotely controlled."[62]

And if that sounds a bit "too James Bond" for you, consider the response from Mr. King:

"We can fly probes to Mars and back by remote control. We fly highly sophisticated spy planes at 60,000 feet without pilots, by remote control. We can certainly take over a car, with the right equipment, and drive that car remotely."[63]

That method has actually been available to elite forces as an assassination technique since the 1980s.[64] It "deploys a microchip transceiver which takes over the target vehicle's steering and brakes at the critical moment."[65]

British Air Marshal Peter Horsley has confirmed that "The Boston Brakes" assassination method has been used in Great Britain and even that *he personally took part in one such operation.*[66]

The exact same characteristics described in that method by Sir Horsley are precisely what took place in the car

---

[62] Everard & Houston, *Lady Die: The Diana Conspiracies*; King & Beveridge, *Princess Diana: The Hidden Evidence*
[63] Ibid.
[64] King & Beveridge, *Princess Diana: The Hidden Evidence*, citing Sir Ranulph Fiennes
[65] King & Beveridge, *Princess Diana: The Hidden Evidence*

[66] Peter Horsley, *Sounds From Another Room* (Pen & Sword Books: 1998)

crash of Lady Diana. "It's *identical* to what happened to the Mercedes in which Diana died."[67]

"All the evidence seems to suggest that that's what happened that night."[68]

If you haven't yet seen the excellent video presentation on "The Boston Brakes" and how it was specifically used on Princess Diana as the assassination technique, that's available online: http://youtu.be/y7ExwQbO5Yc

Former SAS Sergeant, Dave Cornish, spelled it out loud and clear:

"Absolutely. That is exactly how it would have been done. They would have stolen the car, taken one chip out, replaced it with another, no one would have known. That's exactly how it would have been done."[69]

From an intelligence standpoint, the "signature" of the operation was remarkably clear to men like Mr. Cornish:

"From the minute the decoy car left the Ritz to the moment the tail car closed in…it was obvious what was going on."[70]

And here's another professional analysis from a veteran of the Royal Family's personal protection team:

---

67 Everard & Houston, *Lady Die: The Diana Conspiracies*; King & Beveridge, *Princess Diana: The Hidden Evidence*
68 Ibid.
69 Ibid.
70 Richard Coleman, "New Evidence Diana Was Murdered By MI6," citing King & Beveridge, *Princess Diana: The Hidden Evidence*: http://www.consciousape.com/2012/08/21/new-evidence-diana-was-murdered-by-mi6/

"The operation bore all the classic hallmarks of a security service assassination...I have no doubt whatsoever, given my twenty years' experience in various sections of the security industry, that Diana was assassinated. The security service hallmarks are plain to see."[71]

Even the Queen of England reportedly substantiates that theory, amazingly enough.[72] Although it appeared in a tabloid magazine, we're told by intelligence sources not to be so outright dismissive of such stories—operatives often use them to "test out" a story's acceptability, or even to intentionally discredit one by going public with the cover for an operation in a form that the public will reject. So they intentionally leak stories they want people *not* to believe.

According to a report in September 2013, Queen Elizabeth oversaw an investigation that determined who was behind the crash and how it was done. That secret investigation concluded that Diana was indeed murdered and that it was ruthless international arms dealers who were behind it, though it involved former British intelligence agents to carry out the plan; a team of "renegade secret agents from Britain and America and a notorious hit man from Croatia."[73]

That investigation also reportedly concluded:

---

[71] Ibid.
[72] *Globe Magazine*, "The Queen Names Diana's Killers," September 2, 2013: http://www.princess-diana-remembered.com/1/post/2013/08/globe-magazine-september-2nd-2013-the-queen-names-dianas-killers.html
[73] Ibid.

"Her investigators found the limo's brakes and steering had been sabotaged, and that the Croatian villain hid in the tunnel to make sure Diana's driver couldn't keep control by dazzling him with a blinding beam of light."[74]

Don't scoff at the possible involvement of arms dealers in the operation either. There are two excellent books on the subject and they both lead back to the murder of Diana: *Dead Men Don't Eat Lunch* by Geoffrey Gilson and *The Octopus* by Kenn Thomas and Jim Keith.

6. **The Mercedes Had Lost the Paparazzi Pursuers**

The official conclusion was that the Mercedes was speeding into the tunnel to avoid the menace of rapidly pursuing photographers. There's just one problem with that: It isn't true.[75]

What actually happened was that the Al-Fayed security team had fooled most of the paparazzi who were waiting for Diana outside the Ritz Hotel. They had a decoy car in the front of the hotel while Diana and party snuck out the back entrance of the Ritz and into a waiting Mercedes limousine.

The very few paparazzi who had been in *back* of the hotel snapped off their pictures when they saw Diana and that was that. So the paparazzi behind the limo

---

[74] Ibid.
[75] CBS News, "The Truth About The Night Diana Died," July 5, 2010: http://www.cbsnews.com/2100-500185_162-3216431.html

were most definitely *not* immediately behind and encouraging the driver to speed faster to avoid them, as the official version and the media were quick to suggest.

That simply isn't what happened.

There were paparazzi following far back, but they were at least a *full minute* behind the limo.[76]

7. **The Mercedes Was Diverted Into the Tunnel**

The Mercedes left the rear entrance of the Ritz, averting and quickly leaving behind the paparazzi, and then was diverted from its route.[77] Its destination was Dodi's Paris apartment, and to get there after leaving from the back of the Ritz hotel, the obvious and almost only route from there was to take the exit which, in Paris, is known as the "slip route," just prior to coming upon the tunnel.[78]

However, eyewitness testimony established that a vehicle was parked broadside on that small exit slip route and the Mercedes, therefore, was blocked from

---

[76] Sue Reid, "Diana, that SAS murder claim and why it may not be as mad as you think," August 30, 2013, *Daily Mail*: http://www.dailymail.co.uk/news/article-2407571/Princess-Diana-SAS-murder-claim--mad-think-says-SUE-REID.html

[77] Everard & Houston, *Lady Die: The Diana Conspiracies*; King & Beveridge, *Princess Diana: The Hidden Evidence*: http://www.youtube.com/watch?v=ZEojHBs7Nrs

[78] Ibid.

taking it.[79] So the Mercedes changed its route and went down into the tunnel.

This is a very important point as it establishes a planned operation in place to cause the "accident." The Mercedes was diverted into the tunnel. The tunnel was a route that was in the wrong direction for going to their destination (Dodi's apartment). [80]

8. Witnesses Were Observing the Development of the Crash

A reliable eyewitness, French music producer Jacques Morel, established that approximately twelve men were standing inside the tunnel entrance near where the accident occurred. They were in a location where there are usually no people, due to the fact that they had to stand on an extremely narrow pavement—only a foot wide—in harm's way, right next to the rapidly passing traffic. Yet *there were twelve men* there at the time of the incident!

Mr. Morel was driving home with his wife and—before anything happened as far as the crash—he was stunned to see all those men standing there. Here's how he described the bizarre scene:

---

[79] *Princess Diana: The Bizarre Unsolved Disturbing Events Surrounding Her Death*, "Eye Witness Accounts Dispute Official Story," 7-18-2007: http://princess-diana-life-n-death.blogspot.com/2007/07/princess-diana-death-eye-witness.html

[80] Everard & Houston, *Lady Die: The Diana Conspiracies*; King & Beveridge, *Princess Diana: The Hidden Evidence*: http://www.youtube.com/watch?v=y7ExwQbO5Yc

"As we entered the Alma tunnel I looked to my left and saw about a dozen shady figures on a tiny pavement by the side of the opposite carriageway…They were all standing in a long line. The sight was unforgettable. The pavement is less than 30 centimeters wide (about 11 inches) and next to fast traffic. They would have been breathing in petrol fumes and it was very dirty down there. It was certainly not a sensible place to stand around."[81]

What were all those men doing there? It was a very bizarre occurrence taking place precisely at a profoundly important moment.

Other witnesses also noted that a helicopter was hovering overhead before the accident occurred. It's been posited that may have been related to the event, insofar as monitoring events on the ground.[82]

9. **Other Vehicles Then Intentionally Interfered With the Limousine**

Continuing with that planned operational attack, the limousine was then boxed in by other vehicles as it entered the tunnel.

As would be expected of a man entrusted with the personal safety of the Al-Fayed family, Henri Paul was

---

[81] *Princess Diana: The Bizarre Unsolved Disturbing Events Surrounding Her Death*, "Eye Witness Accounts Dispute Official Story"
[82] Mathúna & Heathcote, "The death of Princess Diana: What caused the crash at the Pont d'Alma?"

an excellent driver. In fact, he had recently taken—and successfully completed—special high-performance evasion and protection classes for dignitary protection. They were special classes sponsored by Mercedes-Benz for emergency driving procedures of elite bodyguard and escort units, on how to handle their cars under extreme circumstances such as anti-terrorist and anti-kidnapping evasion techniques.[83]

"Mohamed took his role of self-appointed protector very seriously. All the evidence is that he hired only the very best personnel to act as chauffeurs and bodyguards for his son and the Princess. The cream of Executive Protection specialists. Individuals trained by Governments to protect world leaders, and remove them from harm's way, at a moment's warning. They knew how to bodyguard, and they knew how to drive fast and safely."[84]

A white Fiat Uno had been spotted by an off-duty police officer because it was being driven very erratically.[85]

Upon entering the tunnel, the limo immediately came quickly upon the rear of another vehicle, that same white Fiat Uno.[86]

---

[83] *BBC News Special Report: Diana Remembered*, "The Driver," 10-23-2007:
http://www.bbc.co.uk/news/special/politics97/diana/endingpaul.html
[84] Geoffrey Gilson, *Dead Men Don't Eat Lunch* (Lulu: 2013)
[85] Everard & Houston, *Lady Die: The Diana Conspiracies*; King & Beveridge, *Princess Diana: The Hidden Evidence*:
http://www.youtube.com/watch?v=ZEojHBs7Nrs
[86] Ibid.

The actions of the Fiat Uno were a highly suspicious scenario in itself. It was established by a police officer that it sped towards the tunnel entrance. The Fiat sped by the off-duty police officer, overtaking the vehicle he was driving—and then he noticed that the exact same Fiat was at a virtual standstill, right at the entrance to the tunnel and he thought that was very odd.[87]

Other witnesses confirmed that it then loitered near the entrance to the tunnel, either stopped or traveling unusually slowly.[88]

Then right after the crash, it was identified by a witness, a London attorney who was looking out of his hotel window down at the tunnel where he had just heard two explosions, as speeding out of the tunnel. So it was some very strange from start to finish.

Bear in mind that the drivers of the vehicles on the attack team knew something that the driver of the limousine did not know until the last minute: they knew that the car was going to be forced to enter down into the tunnel. And at that point—with other vehicles operationally in place—they were more in control of what happened to the Mercedes limo than was its driver.

So the Fiat, as eyewitness testimony confirms, entered the tunnel just as the Mercedes was approaching. When the Mercedes had its planned exit diverted and went down into the tunnel, it quickly came upon the slow-moving Fiat immediately in front of it and was forced to veer sharply to get around it. At that time—

---

[87] Ibid.
[88] Ibid.

according to eyewitness testimony—another slow-moving sedan was in front of the limo in that lane, boxing it in, and a motorcycle with two riders aboard it passed the limousine on its left.[89]

Some witnesses stated that there several motorcycles, but it's very clear that there was *at least* one, with two riders aboard. The limousine then swerved sharply, which was caused by a motorcycle overtaking it at high speed on the left side of the limo and a braking vehicle in front of the Mercedes that boxed it in.

The eyewitness testimony substantiates the above scenario. The following are statements from witnesses to the scene:

"The crash came when the car…swerved sharply in the tunnel to avoid a vehicle which suddenly loomed ahead."

"There are two separate witnesses…that a car driving IN FRONT OF, the Mercedes S280, forced the Mercedes to start braking, as it entered the tunnel."

"The Mercedes was driving on the right hand, shortly before the entry of the tunnel, preceded by a dark-colored automobile, of which make I cannot say. This car clearly was attempting to force the Mercedes to brake...The driver of the Mercedes veered into the left-hand lane, and then entered the tunnel."

---

[89] Reid, "Diana, that SAS murder claim and why it may not be as mad as you think": http://www.dailymail.co.uk/news/article-2407571/Princess-Diana-SAS-murder-claim--mad-think-says-SUE-REID.html

"A motorbike with two men forced me off the road. It was following a big car."

"I noticed one of the motorcycles going and attempting to pass on the left side of the car."

"I saw the motorcycle get over and begin like he was going through the passing movement . . . I did see motorcycles. Two, three people - one single and one with two people and the one with the two people was the one that actually tried to make, getting between the left hand side."

"It was a powerful black car, I think a Mercedes…This car was clearly being pursued by several motorcycles, I would say four to six of them. Some were mounted by two riders. These motorcycles were tailing the vehicle and some tried to pull up alongside it.

"I saw the car in the middle of the tunnel with the motorcycle on its left, pulling ahead and then swerving to the right directly in front of the car."

I "saw a motorcycle swerve directly in front of the Mercedes, making it lose control."[90]

So the above accounts, taken in totality, establish how the Mercedes was literally attacked by a group of vehicles. The scene was clearly one of a quickly occurring and highly calculated chaos.

---

[90] Ibid.

An important determination at the crime scene was that the Fiat Uno didn't leave skid marks; meaning that it didn't quickly come to a stop as one would think it would after witnessing a horrific accident. In fact, it didn't stop at all. The Fiat raced out of the tunnel.[91]

Many have speculated that the driver of the Fiat Uno was a man named James Andanson. James Andanson was a photographer and MI6 informant. It's been established that he did indeed own a white Fiat Uno, identical to the one in the crash, although it has not been proven to a certainty that his car was the one in the tunnel.[92] But it *has* been established that Mr. Andanson boasted to friends that he was in the tunnel when Diana was killed.[93]

Mr. Andanson was later murdered. *Legally* speaking, he committed suicide. That was the official ruling. But take our word for it on this one—he was murdered. He was found in a remote location, a firefighter said he was positive that he saw two bullet holes in his head, and his body was burned beyond recognition, in a car that he was locked in and the car was locked *from the outside*—yet there were *no car keys* at the crime scene.[94] Think about *that* one for a while.

---

91 Everard & Houston, *Lady Die: The Diana Conspiracies*; http://www.youtube.com/watch?v=d6ydFXtc74U
92 Everard & Houston, *Lady Die: The Diana Conspiracies*; http://www.youtube.com/watch?v=1b4usGUhAOc
93 *Whale*, "New Witness Evidence…retrieved 10-9-2013: http://www.whale.to/b/pap1.html
94 *Whale*, "New Witness Evidence …"; Martin Evans, "Diana: Fiat driver…," July 9, 7=-9-2007, *Express UK*: http://www.express.co.uk/news/uk/12839/Diana-Fiat-driver-shot-in-the-head;

Veteran investigative journalists like Jon King have pieced together a great deal about the mysterious Mr. Andanson:

"What we know is he was almost certainly in the tunnel. What we know is he witnessed the crash, he took photos of the crash, he took photos of whoever was there immediately after the crash. He must have seen that Fiat Uno, whether he was driving it or not. He must have seen who was on the motorbike that overtook the Mercedes immediately before it crashed. So he had some *very* compromising photographs."[95]

But it appears that Mr. Andanson was more of a scapegoat than a killer. While he may have sold information to MI6 over the years, he was not actually the type of person to be contracted as an assassin on such a high-profile and sophisticated operation.[96]

John McNamara, formerly a veteran Senior Detective and then Chief of Security for the Al-Fayed family, investigated the whole Fiat matter and concluded that the French authorities were not the least bit interested in the fact that McNamara's investigators had found the white Fiat and proved that it had the damage replaced after the accident, was then painted, and quickly sold. Nor were they interested in the fact that Andanson's office was broken into and his work was stolen

---

[95] *SteelMagnolia*, "James Andanson Murdered by a Yugoslav Code-Named 'T' Connected to Intelligence Agencies," December 31, 2011, citing French newspaper *Le Investigateu*, dossier "France": http://dianaunlawfullkilling.blogspot.com/2011/12/james-andanson-murdered-by-yogoslav.html
[96] Ibid.

concurrent with his death, which was obviously a murder and not a suicide.[97]

Mr. McNamara is not a man to be taken lightly, and he summed up the situation quite succinctly:

"You have a Mercedes that's done a 180 degree turn, having crashed into the thirteenth pillar and yet the Fiat Uno survives everything, which suggests to me that that was a very professional driver. I can well believe, as a detective with 24 years' experience, why Mr. Al- Fayed believes that his son Dodi and Princess Diana were murdered."[98]

10. **A High-Intensity Light Was Witnessed in the Tunnel**

The eyewitness testimony also clearly established another disturbing fact. Many people saw an extremely bright strobe-like flash just prior to the crash, and described it as coming from the motorcycle. The witnesses specifically noted that the flash was far too bright and intense to have been from the camera of a flash photographer.

Therefore, the implication is that, as the motorcycle passed the limousine, it flashed some type of hi-tech strobe light device which caused the crash by either

---

[97] *Whale*, "New Witness Evidence Proves That Paparazzo James Andanson Was Shot In The Head," retrieved October 9, 2013: http://www.whale.to/b/pap1.html
[98] Ibid.

blinding the driver or knocking out the car's computerized control systems, or both.

Witness testimony indicates that "when the bike was 15 feet in front of the car there was a fierce flash of white light which came from the motorbike."[99]

Note the way that witnesses described it:

"a blinding flash of light, much brighter and far more intense than any camera flash"[100]

"an enormous radar-like flash of light"[101]

"As it swerved there was a flash of light. It was an explosion of light. Like a searchlight."[102]

Those remarks are clearly not in reference to a camera flash.

Here are some of the statements from eyewitnesses in the tunnel:

"I saw the car in the middle of the tunnel with the motorcycle on its left, pulling ahead and then swerving to the right directly in front of the car…as the

---

[99] Reid, "Diana, that SAS murder claim and why it may not be as mad as you think"
[100] King & Beveridge, *Princess Diana: The Hidden Evidence*, 20.
[101] *Newsmine*, "Diana Crash 'Caused By Laser Beam'," 6-02-2006, citing *Daily Express UK*: http://newsmine.org/content.php?ol=deceptions/assassinations/princess-diana/diana-crash-caused-by-laser-beam.txt
[102] Noel Botham, *The Murder of Princess Diana* (Pinnacle: 2004), citing witness Levistre.

motorcycle swerved and before the car lost control, there was a flash of light…"[103]

"A motorbike with two men forced me off the road. It was following a big car. Afterwards in the tunnel there were very strong lights like flashes. After that, a black car arrived. The big car had come off the road."[104]

"…as the motorcycle swerved and before the car lost control, there was a flash of light…"[105]

"The light was very powerful…a major white flash…It came into my car. The light was not directed towards me. It was directed towards the car which was behind."

"There was an almighty bang and a great big flash of light."[106]

The intensity of that "great big flash of light" has never been sufficiently explained. As the driver of a car near the Mercedes concluded, it certainly wasn't from a camera, and it happened *before* the car crashed:

"He concluded that the intensity of the flash was much greater than that produced by a normal photographer's flash."[107]

---

[103] Mathúna & Heathcote, "Eyewitness accounts …"
[104] Ibid.
[105] Ibid.
[106] *Princess Diana: The Bizarre Unsolved Disturbing Events Surrounding Her Death*, "Eye Witness Accounts Dispute Official Story," 6-18-2007: http://princess-diana-life-n-death.blogspot.com/2007/07/princess-diana-death-eye-witness.html
[107] Richard Palmer, "Diana sensation: 'I saw hit man cause crash'," October 16, 2007: http://www.express.co.uk/news/uk/22196/Diana-sensation-I-saw-hitman-cause-crash

11. **An Explosion Was Heard and the Limousine "Went Dark" Prior to the Crash**

Several eyewitness reports specifically noted that there was a huge explosion in the tunnel *before* the car crashed into the pillar. That's of huge importance because it's an obvious indication of some type of explosive device—and hence, *murder*—that the vehicle was subjected to.

Witnesses say they heard "an explosion and then a bang."[108]

Joana Luz was an American tourist who witnessed the crash:

"We were walking along the Seine river and we heard a huge explosion. It sounded like a huge gunshot. We knew it was a screech (of tires) and then a—it sounded like an explosion and after that we heard another screech and another hard explosion and it sounded like a car crash."[109]

Mohamed Medjahdi was in a car inside the tunnel. He said:

"The limousine was "slewing across the carriageway completely out of control (and) accelerated away just before a loud explosion and the limousine crashed into a pillar."[110]

---

[108] Mathúna & Heathcote, "The death of Princess Diana: What caused the crash at the Pont d'Alma?"
[109] *BBC*, "In Their Own Words," retrieved 10-11-2013: http://www.bbc.co.uk/news/special/politics97/diana/diquotes.html
[110] Penny Thornton, "Diana, In Memoriam," 8-31-2007: http://www.astrolutely.com/articles-9-Diana-In-Memoriam

"It was a dreadful sound, like a bomb exploding, magnified and echoing around the underpass. Even today, six years later, I can't get the sight and sound out of my head. I can still hear the screeching of those brakes."[111]

So the important point to note is that the "loud explosion" took place *before* the limousine crashed.

Some of the witnesses described a series of sounds. Businessman Gary Dean:

"I heard a short, sharp sound followed by a thud, then a massive impact followed by two other thuds."[112]

It was also reported that the Mercedes emitted a strange "whooshing sound" prior to the crash:

"It was traveling very fast and gave off a whooshing noise as it entered the tunnel as if the driver had hit the clutch but failed to change gear."

That strange sound also could have had some relation to a takeover of the car's computerized control system, the point we discussed earlier regarding "The Boston Brakes" assassination technique.

"The witness said that what drew his attention to the scene, was the loud sound of the Mercedes' gears being suddenly lowered. The other witness, who was walking

---

[111] *active-world*, "Diana: The Chronology Collated," 3-08-2007: http://archive-world-nour-obscur.blogspot.com/2007/03/diana-chronology-collated.html

[112] *Diana Remembered,* "Di inquest pregnancy rumours," citing *The Sun*, retrieved 10-10-2013: http://dianaremembered.wordpress.com/2007/10/17/di-inquest-pregnancy-rumours/

along the riverside, said he was surprised by the 'sound of a motor humming very loudly.'"[113]

There is also an eyewitness report, again from the reliable witness, Jacques Morel, that the Mercedes "went dark" prior to the crash. That is yet another indication of the car's computerized systems being affected:

"And then the car had no lights any more. Everything was switched off."[114]

12. **The Kill-Team Even Stopped and Verified That Target Was Hit**

As if there wasn't enough suspicious activity going on in that tunnel, get a load of this one:

The motorcycle stopped after the crash and one of the men got off the bike, walked over to the car and "verified the kill." Both men were dressed in all black. The one who got off the motorcycle and went over and looked into the limousine, then looked over at the other man on the motorcycle and signaled him with the "Mission Accomplished" military sign.[115]

We kid you not. The event was witnessed. Here's what happened:

---

[113] *active-world*, "Diana: The Chronology Collated"
[114] Palmer, "Diana sensation: 'I saw hit man cause crash'"
[115] Reid, "Diana, that SAS murder claim and why it may not be as mad as you think"

"They were dressed in all black with helmets. And the passenger went to the car, looked into the car – because from my mirror I could see everything that was happening – and the passenger he made a gesture with his hands." The witness then crossed his lowered arms to demonstrate the sign indicating that it was all over.

The witness then told the Court how the man in black then signaled that they needed to hurry out of the tunnel. He quickly got back on the motorcycle and the two men roared off out of the tunnel.

The Court then asked him:

"Was there any reason you didn't get out of the car?"

"Fear. It's just like I said to the magistrates before, I thought they were hitmen."[116]

And it sounds like he was right, doesn't it?

13. **The Accident Was Survivable**

Even *without* her seatbelt strapped, Diana's wounds were very survivable. She was *not* pinned in the vehicle, as was erroneously reported. The doctor who stopped to help her and was first medical personnel at the scene, was confident that she would be okay. He surveyed the damage, noted that she was both conscious and speaking, and then he handed over her care to the emergency personnel upon their arrival, as per protocol. But he stated that he left that scene very confident that

---

[116] Palmer, "Diana sensation: 'I saw hit man cause crash'"

she would survive. And as we will document, he was quite right about that assumption—Diana *should* have survived.

Dr. Frederic Maillez had seen the accident occur and immediately got out of his car and went over to help. He surveyed the damage; he moved Diana's head to make sure that she could breathe, and then he called the emergency hotline on his cell phone.[117] On the phone, he told them the exact location, the fact that the driver and rear passenger behind him appeared to be dead but that there were two survivors, and he requested two ambulances and a rescue vehicle in case anyone was trapped.[118] He was told that ambulances were already on the way.[119]

Then he got an oxygen mask from his car and he treated Diana. He made sure that she was not going to choke, not going to swallow her tongue, that she was conscious, and then he administered oxygen. He noted, as a later doctor on the scene *also* noted, that her vital signs indicated that she was bleeding internally. But he was confident that she would be quickly brought to a hospital, so when the physician in the emergency ambulance arrived, he handed over her care to that doctor, just as protocol directs. But he felt confident she would survive.

---

[117] Jeffrey Steinberg & Allen Douglas, "French cover-up of Diana assassination exposed!," November 21, 1997, *EIR Investigation*, Vol. 24, No. 47: http://www.larouchepub.com/eiw/public/1997/eirv24n47-19971121/eirv24n47-19971121_048-french_cover_up_of_diana_assassi.pdf

[118] *active-world*, "Diana: The Chronology Collated"

[119] Steinberg & Douglas, "French cover-up of Diana assassination exposed!"

As another doctor at the crash scene confirmed:

"She was sweating and her blood pressure had dropped.

She had the external signs of internal hemorrhage."[120]

Carlo Zaglia was an off-duty fireman and was also one of the first people on the scene to assist the victims. Mr. Zaglia comforted Diana:

"She could speak, she could hear and her eyes were open."[121] He said she was even trying to stand up.[122]

So the facts are clear:

- Diana survived the crash;
- Diana was conscious after the crash;
- Diana was speaking, after the crash;
- Diana was not pinned in the vehicle;
- It was assumed by the first doctor at the scene that Diana would be okay;
- It was a noted observation by at least two of the first physicians at the crash scene that Diana was exhibiting the signs of internal bleeding;
- As medical personnel are trained in and keenly aware of, the only treatment for internal bleeding is surgery at a hospital to stop the bleeding.

---

[120] Ibid.
[121] *active-world*, "Diana: The Chronology Collated"
[122] Ibid.

Professor Murray MacKay is Britain's premier accident investigator and a recognized expert in the scientific analysis of crash dynamics, concluded that the Mercedes was only traveling at no more than 60-to-63 mph when it struck the pillar. His methods of scientific analysis further determined from skid marks and other evidence at the crash scene, that the Mercedes then came away from the pillar at an exit speed of 10 mph. Professor MacKay determined that the change in velocity was slightly less than 50 mph and therefore, highly survivable:

"This was a severe but survivable accident."[123]

14. **It Took 100 Precious Minutes to Get Diana to the Hospital**

One would think that, under *any* circumstances, a crash victim suffering from internal bleeding would be brought quickly to one of several nearby hospitals equipped with trauma centers for *precisely* such situations. One would think it all the more if the crash victim was a high-profile personality and world-recognized person like Princess Diana.

Well, guess what, class? *Not so.*

Diana died during a needlessly long journey to one of those hospitals.

---

[123] King & Beveridge, *Princess Diana: The Hidden Evidence*; Everard & Houston, *Lady Die: The Diana Conspiracies*

"One highly respected French doctor who specializes in emergency response, told EIR, in an exclusive interview, that Princess Diana should have been taken to the Val de Grace, 'which is much closer than La Pitie. That is a military hospital. Every political figure who is in a car crash or is injured is taken there.' The doctor added: 'The firemen, who were on the scene of the crash, are part of the Army. They undoubtedly notified the Val de Grace, which has a top team of trauma specialists on duty 'round the clock. I might have helicoptered her in. She would have been on the operating block a few minutes after being stabilized. This woman was one of the world's most powerful and influential people. She would normally have been given top priority and top treatment. She was not.'"[124]

A re-enactment of the ambulance journey—at *rush* hour, in *bad* weather, and with *no* police escort—only took 11 minutes. It should have only taken Diana's ambulance somewhere between 5-to-10 minutes. But the ambulance took 40 minutes to make that journey.

Dr. Martino ordered the driver to stop and park, outside a history museum, because Diana was in critical condition. The ambulance waited there even though the hospital was within view of their location—less than a two-minute walk. No emergency personnel made that two-minute journey, even though the ambulance was within view of the emergency entrance of the hospital

[124] Steinberg & Douglas, "French cover-up of Diana assassination exposed!"

and emergency personnel there were on standby awaiting the wounded Princess Diana.[125]

That's all the more bizarre when you consider that it was an extremely high-profile case—I mean *geez,* it's only the world-famous Royal Princess in need of urgent medical attention: *hell-o,* anybody out there?—and the hospital staff had been alerted of her impending arrival.

But nobody can just walk out to the ambulance to see if they need any help when it's totally freaking apparent that they *obviously* need some help or wouldn't be unable to get to the emergency room! Can you believe that?

THE SLOW JOURNEY TO DIANA'S DEATH FROM INTERNAL BLEEDING

TIMELINE[126]

12:25am The accident occurs in the tunnel

12:26am Dr. Maillez stops to help and calls in the emergency.

12:28am Doctor Maillez finds an off-duty firefighter already assisting victims and he administers oxygen to a conscious Princess Diana.

---

[125] Everard & Houston, *Lady Die: The Diana Conspiracies*
[126] "Timeline: How Diana Died," BBC News, 12-14-2006: http://news.bbc.co.uk/2/hi/programmes/conspiracy_files/6217366.stm

12:32am The first emergency crew, a military emergency service, arrives and takes over from Dr. Maillez.

12:40am The French SAMU ambulance ("Service d'Aide Médicale Urgente" or Urgent Medical Aid Service) arrives with an on-board physician. They remove Diana from the Mercedes, treat her at roadside, put her on an IV drip, then place her in the ambulance.

1:25am Diana has now been at the crash site for 1 full hour as the medical unit from the ambulance team continues to treat her in the tunnel. She was *not* pinned in the car. She was removed from the car and treated in the ambulance. But the ambulance remained stationary in the tunnel instead of proceeding to a nearby trauma center, less than five minutes away. At 1:25, the ambulance finally leaves for the hospital. But even with a police escort, it travels at only 25 miles per hour. It neglects to go to any of five other hospitals equipped with trauma centers which are all closer, because it has been directed to go to La Pitie Salpetriere Hospital, which is probably better—unless you happen to be bleeding to death at the time.

1:55am The ambulance stops—within sight of the hospital—to treat Diana for a drop in blood pressure. It sits there for 10 minutes, parked outside the French Natural History Museum—only a few hundred yards away from the hospital.[127]

2:06am It is now over 1 hour, 40 minutes from the crash. The 4-mile journey that would only take 5 minutes to travel normally in a car has now taken an ambulance, assisted with

---

[127] "French cover-up of Diana assassination exposed!," Jeffrey Steinberg & Allen Douglas, 11-21-1997, *EIR Investigation*, Vol. 24, No. 47: http://www.larouchepub.com/eiw/public/1997/eirv24n47-19971121/eirv24n47-19971121_048-french_cover_up_of_diana_assassi.pdf

two police escorts, a minimum of 41 minutes (by some estimates, several minutes longer). The ambulance finally arrives at the hospital.

4:05am Diana is pronounced dead after various efforts to revive her fail. Cardiac arrest is the technical diagnosis, but it is the result of massive blood loss from internal hemorrhaging. She literally bled to death.[128]

As the UK newspaper *The Scotsman* observed:

"What is puzzling about the treatment offered to Diana is that she was not hospitalized until her condition had deteriorated to a critical extent. She suffered a series of heart attacks in the tunnel and on the way to the hospital, and had a massive cardiac arrest within minutes of arriving at La Pitie Salpetriere. The truth is that she was dead on arrival in the operating theater, although the surgical team battled against all the odds to revive her. No convincing explanation has been offered for the delay. The surgical team at the hospital had a long time in which to prepare for the arrival of their patient. They were in telephone communication with the doctors in the tunnel from the very beginning and were on formal alert from 1 a.m."[129]

"The decision to bring Princess Diana to La Pitie Salpetriere Hospital was evidently made by the senior French government officials on the spot, Paris Police Chief Massoni and Interior Minister Chevenement.

---

[128] "Diana: The Chronology Collated," *active-world*, 3-08-2007: http://archive-world-nour-obscur.blogspot.com/2007/03/diana-chronology-collated.html

[129] Steinberg & Douglas, "French cover-up of Diana assassination exposed!," citing *The Scotsman*

Massoni was in the tunnel, and Chevenement was already at La Pitie Salpetriere, in phone contact with the rescue crew in the tunnel. Yet, there are five other hospitals closer to the crash site, all with advanced emergency capabilities."[130]

So here it is, folks, plain and ugly:

"The SAMU team spent nearly an hour, until 1:30 a.m. treating Diana in the tunnel. Then the ambulance drove her at a snail's pace to Piete-Salpetriere hospital, 6.15 kilometers away. At that time of night, it would normally take five or 10 minutes to do that drive along the riverfront expressway. But Diana's driver, applying standard French emergency procedures, drove extremely slowly so as not to subject the fragile patient to shocks and bumps. As a result, it took them some 40 minutes to make the drive, and the ambulance stopped within a few hundred yards of the hospital to treat a sharp drop in blood pressure."[131]

And here is the disposition of Diana's wounds from a medical standpoint:

"By the time Diana reached the emergency room, it was nearly an hour and 45 minutes after the crash. According to the deposition of the on-duty doctor, who admitted her into the hospital, she arrived alive and

---

[130] Ibid.

[131] Thomas A. Sancton D. Phil. Oxon., "Death Of A Princess, Did Princess Diana Have To Die?: A Case Study In French Emergency Medicine," *The Internet Journal of Rescue and Disaster Medicine*, 2000, Vol. 1, No. 2: http://archive.ispub.com/journal/the-internet-journal-of-rescue-and-disaster-medicine/volume-1-number-2/death-of-a-princess-did-princess-diana-have-to-die-a-case-study-in-french-emergency-medicine.html#sthash.xvRa2aam.dpbs

with a cardiac rhythm. Though she had no serious external injuries, X-rays indicated internal hemorrhaging that was compressing her right lung and heart. Within 10 minutes of her arrival, the patient again suffered a cardiac arrest, prompting the doctors to inject large doses of epinephrine directly into the heart, and to perform an emergency thoracotomy."[132]

And here it is medically, regarding the moment of death:

"According to testimony of the chief surgeon on duty that night, the operation revealed that the source of the hemorrhaging was a single lesion, which he described as a partial rupture of the left pulmonary vein at the point of contact with the left atrium. The tear was sutured and the hemorrhaging was stopped. But despite nearly two hours of manual internal massage, and the application of electroshocks, it was impossible to reestablish a heartbeat. The patient was declared death at 4 a.m."[133]

So by the time they finally got her to the emergency room it was 1 hour and 40 minutes after the crash and it was too late. She died from the internal bleeding that can only be stopped by surgery. Which is *precisely why* emergency medical protocol is to <u>rush</u> an internally bleeding victim to a trauma center. Her life clearly could have been saved had they done so. There were even other trauma center-equipped hospitals that were *closer* than the one they crawled at a snail's pace to. It's true that in France the medical protocol differs from

---

[132] Ibid.
[133] Ibid.

the United States and they attempt to treat the victim at the scene first. But in this case, that ridiculous delay cost the victim her life.

In 2000, a respected medical journal did a very scientific study on whether, from a standpoint of medical treatment, Diana could have been saved. They reached the obvious conclusion: yes.

Please read that medical study (the website can be found at the bottom of this page) and you will see that, from a treating physician's standpoint, her death from that crash was completely avoidable.[134]

Any way you look at it, Diana's life would have been saved if they had rushed her to a trauma center, and there was one was one that ready and waiting for her, less than five minutes away. But it took them 1 hour and 40 minutes to get her there, so she bled to death.

THE COVER-UP

The official version of Diana's death is that the driver of her limousine was drunk and the fact that the limousine was being pursued by paparazzi made him drive recklessly and lose control of the car, crashing it into a pillar.

Nice try. Except that the only part of that version that's true is part that the car crashed into a pillar. He wasn't drunk, nor was the paparazzi close to their car.

---

[134] Thomas A. Sancton D. Phil. Oxon., "Death Of A Princess, Did Princess Diana Have To Die?" *The Internet Journal of Rescue and Disaster Medicine*, 2000, Vol. 1, No. 2

PRESS CARS WERE NOT CLOSE TO THE LIMOUSINE

It is well-established in the evidence that the paparazzi were most definitely *not* close to the limousine at the moment of the crash. The surprise exit out the back of the Ritz actually did fool the press corps and members of the press did not catch up with the Mercedes limo until *after* it crashed in the tunnel. That fact is documented in the records by the testimony of those were first to arrive at the crash scene.[135]

HENRI PAUL WAS NOT DRUNK

Although the official conclusion of the British investigation was that Henri Paul was drunk, that determination appears to be a total invention.[136]

In fact, Lord Stevens, the head of that investigation, even sat down with Henri Paul's parents and conceded to them both that their son had not been drunk and that he had only two alcoholic drinks.[137] Numerous eyewitness, as well as bills and records from the Ritz bar, substantiate the fact that—beyond question—all that Mr. Paul had that evening was two drinks.[138]

---

[135] King & Beveridge, *Princess Diana: The Hidden Evidence*; Everard & Houston, *Lady Die: The Diana Conspiracies*
[136] Reid, "Diana, that SAS murder claim and why it may not be as mad as you think"
[137] Ibid.
[138] Ibid.

Further to the facts of the matter, Henri Paul was not just some last-minute call-in to drive the Mercedes, as some articles in mainstream media have implied. He was an excellent driver and security expert:

"Henri Paul had worked for the Fayeds for 11 years and was, according to their spokesman, Michael Cole, an 'exemplary employee'.

He had twice been to Stuttgart in Germany on courses run by Mercedes-Benz on how to handle their cars; these included anti-terrorist and anti-kidnapping evasion techniques."[139]

It's well-established that the Al-Fayed family knew and trusted Henri Paul. As Chief of Security at the esteemed Paris Ritz Hotel, Henri Paul was known as competent and capable of performing those duties. And the presence of Princess Diana actually *enhanced* security protocols in place for her protection:

"Mohamed al-Fayed was more than aware of Diana's longstanding run-in with the paparazzi, and went out of his way to ensure that, whenever she was with Dodi, she was fully 'protected.' This was one of the reasons that Diana enjoyed her time with the Fayeds – she had space and solitude."[140]

"Indeed, Trevor Rees-Jones, the British bodyguard in the front passenger seat of the car in the crash, had served time with both the British Parachute Regiment

---

[139] *BBC News Special Report: Diana Remembered*, "The Driver," 10-23-2007: http://www.bbc.co.uk/news/special/politics97/diana/endingpaul.html

[140] Geoffrey Gilson, *Dead Men Don't Eat Lunch* (Lulu: 2013)

and the Royal Protection Squad. Even though Henri Paul may not have had similar elite training, there is simply no way al-Fayed would have endangered either his son or his meal ticket by entrusting them to the driving of someone he knew to be a drunk."[141]

Samples also revealed that there were significant levels of Prozac (a strong anti-depressant) that *further increases* the effects of alcohol and should not be taken at the same time. That point makes it impossible that no one noticed anything odd about Henri's behavior and allowed him to drive. If he had mixed significant amounts of Prozac with enough alcohol to place him at 3 times over the legal limit, there's no way it would have gone unnoticed in the context of Dignitary Protection.

Yet there is a security tape video of him tying both his shoes shortly before the crash and he succeeds in doing that, with no problem whatsoever. Mr. Al-Fayed released all the security footage from the Ritz Hotel that evening, purposefully revealing a quite sober Henri Paul. He can clearly be seen, thirty minutes prior to the crash, squatting and tying his shoelaces. "He transfers his weight gracefully from left to right, and gets up again, without a hitch or stumble."[142]

You can watch that film footage online: http://youtu.be/_q6P2M8j_uo

"There is no indication from any of the video tapes of Henri Paul in the short time he was in the Ritz Hotel,

---

141 Ibid.

142 "Henri Paul – Rare CCTV Footage," retrieved 9-05-2013: http://www.youtube.com/watch?v=_q6P2M8j_uo

before leaving with Dodi and Diana in the Mercedes, that he was on any sort of 'high.' Plus, if Henri Paul was on both Prozac and alcohol, as is being suggested, and he had done this before, as is also being suggested, either he would have known what the effect would be, or one of his co-workers in the Hotel would have witnessed it happening to him."[143]

The two bodyguards nearest Henri Paul that night—Trevor Rees-Jones and Alexander "Kes" Wingfield—both stated that Henri was not drunk, and both testified to that under oath. They were both professional and responsible members of an elite dignitary protection team. Mr. Rees-Jones has also pointed out that if the driver had been going too fast then he *would have told him so* and, likewise, if he had observed the chauffeur inebriated or in any way incapable of the necessary requirements of their situation then he *would have done something about it.* He was well aware that this the Princess of Wales they were protecting, as well as an Al-Fayed, and he was all eyes and all ears on task to that duty—Dodi Al-Fayed was Trevor Rees-Jones' personal charge and he took his job very seriously. And he and Kes Wingfield had both been in the presence of the driver, Henri Paul, prior to the trip. Henri Paul was head of Ritz security and they were actually in his presence.[144]

So it does not look at all like the official version would like us to think it was—it was most emphatically not personal error.

---

[143] Gilson, *Dead Men Don't Eat Lunch*
[144] King & Beveridge, *Princess Diana: The Hidden Evidence*; Everard & Houston, *Lady Die: The Diana Conspiracies*

THE BLOOD SAMPLES HAD TO HAVE BEEN FALSIFIED

The blood samples attributed to the driver, Henri Paul, contained absurdly high levels of carbon monoxide. The 21% level of carbon monoxide in the blood sample is quite lethal. That's a fatal level. So it's impossible that it's accurate; because the security footage at the Paris Ritz that night vividly demonstrates a sober Henri Paul, walking, interacting and tying his shoelaces with no difficulty whatsoever.[145]

That has led to speculation—and direct charges from the investigation of the Al-Fayed family—that the samples attributed to Henri Paul were actually taken from another body. Authors Jon King and John Beveridge have established that the blood sample of Henri Paul—upon which the verdict of the court was actually based—was never DNA-identified, that it was taken from a vial labeled "Unknown male" and that it contained such an excessive level of carbon monoxide that:

"Six of the world's most eminent forensic experts stated under oath that it could not possibly have belonged to Henri Paul."[146]

---

[145] Ibid.

[146] Richard Coleman, "New Evidence Diana Was Murdered By MI6," citing King & Beveridge, *Princess Diana: The Hidden Evidence*: http://www.consciousape.com/2012/08/21/new-evidence-diana-was-murdered-by-mi6/

Legal efforts by the Al-Fayed family have failed to force French authorities to reveal the identities of the other bodies which were in the morgue at the same time as Henri Paul.

The point is that it would have been extremely convenient to take a blood sample from one of the vagrants in the morgue to "substantiate" a higher level of alcohol content in the driver. That might sound dubious after first, until one considers the fact of the outrageously high carbon monoxide level also found in the blood. That level cannot be explained otherwise and reportedly one of the other bodies in the morgue at that time was a vagrant with an extremely high alcohol level who died from carbon monoxide poisoning.

The authorities attempted to explain away the carbon monoxide level by "explaining" that it came out of the air bags. However, Dodi Al-Fayed did not have any carbon monoxide in his blood. Henri Paul died instantly in the crash so the carbon monoxide would not have entered his bloodstream anyway.

And just to put the icing on the cake, Mercedes-Benz was contacted and they verified that there is no carbon monoxide content whatsoever in the airbags of their Mercedes.[147]

DIANA WAS NOT PINNED IN THE VEHICLE

---

[147] Ibid.

The falsehood that Diana's body was stuck inside the car was apparently invented in a futile attempt at justifying the fact that it took almost two hours to get her to a hospital.

"Contrary to stories leaked by French authorities to the press, she was not pinned in the rear compartment. The back seat of the Mercedes had not been seriously damaged in the crash, and there was no obstruction to getting at Diana. The French authorities issued these initial false reports in response to queries why it had taken an incredible one hour and 43 minutes, from the time that the first ambulance arrived at the crash site, to deliver Princess Diana to the hospital—four miles away."[148]

THE SECURITY CAMERAS IN THE TUNNEL DID NOT WORK ON THE NIGHT OF THE CRASH

Mohamed Al-Fayed, owner of the Paris Ritz Hotel and father of Diana's boyfriend, Dodi, released the security camera film footage of events in the Ritz to the public so that we could see that actual events contradicted the official version. We'll go over that in detail in the Cover-Up section. It's very revealing and that footage details important events that took place just prior to the crash.

---

[148] Steinberg & Douglas, "French cover-up of Diana assassination exposed!"

But you may be wondering what happened to the traffic film footage of the crash itself and the events just prior to it. So were we! Well, guess what? There isn't any!

And that's rather strange because, as NBC noted, Paris is a city possessing the "most sophisticated video surveillance system of any city in the world"—its traffic cameras record to video tape and those tapes, even under typical circumstances, are saved for two days.[149] Except on this particular occasion—the death of a member of the Royal Family—and we are told to believe that no one bothered to get those tapes. Preposterous? Yep—That's a pretty good way to put it.

The streets of Paris are clustered with video cameras—there are *seventeen video cameras* in the Pont de l'Alma tunnel (where the crash took place) and *another ten* cameras that should have tracked the Mercedes' approach to that tunnel for a total of *twenty-seven surveillance cameras*![150] That footage *should* have shown us a vivid video timeline of Diana's limousine on the fatal route. But we are told that no film footage exists.

"Mohamed Al-Fayed's lawyers requested that the French authorities submit all the CCTV video tapes from the seventeen cameras that covered Diana's journey from the Ritz hotel to the tunnel. The French authorities stated that no such videos existed, as there

---

[149] Seán Mac Mathúna, "The traffic camera at the Pont d'Alma," 2000: http://www.fantompowa.net/Flame/diana_traffic_camera.htm
[150] *The Death of Princess Diana,* 5-26-2010: http://www.y2kprep.com/2010/05/26/the-death-of-princess-diana/

was a power outage and none of the cameras were working for 25 minutes."[151]

Isn't that just a little bit too convenient? You'd have to be pretty naïve to just write that off to coincidence, wouldn't you?

So here's one beauty of a question for you: Why were the CCTV cameras in the tunnel not working? Isn't that just like a movie? The first thing the hi-tech crooks do is disable the video surveillance.

Oddly, there are *other* reports that indicate that the cameras *were* working. For example, there's an apparently valid report of a Parisian driver who received a traffic citation based on CCTV footage, for speeding in the same tunnel where authorities said the cameras were not working.[152] That was mere minutes before the crash of the Mercedes with Diana, according to a 2006 newspaper report.[153]

So either they were turned off, or they were seized and then "disappeared" like the surveillance tapes at the Pentagon mysteriously did on 9/11. Either way you look at it, it means somebody did *not* want that surveillance footage to see the light of the day. Isn't that just a tad bit suspicious?

---

[151] Vince M. Lewis, *The Conspiracy Zone: Conspiracy Theories Exploring Hidden Truth* (Dorrance Publishing: 2013)
[152] *Unexplained-Mysteries.com*, "CCTV was working in the tunnel Diana died in," March 6, 2006: http://www.unexplained-mysteries.com/forum/index.php?showtopic=63492
[153] Ibid.

THE CRIME SCENE WAS IMMEDIATELY CONTAMINATED

Well, here's another one: How about destroying evidence at the scene of the crime? It was more than just the oddity of the surveillance cameras malfunctioning.

"If this seems strange, so, too, was Paris officials' decision to send the green vehicles of its cleansing department into the tunnel only seven hours after the crash. Their efficiency at spraying the whole area with disinfectant expunged forever all forensic evidence remaining at the crash site."[154]

Great job, guys. *That a way,* boys, to preserve the most important crime scene in the last fifty years. Way to go.

MERCEDES BENZ' OFFERS TO ASSIST IN THE INVESTIGATION WERE REBUFFED

Mercedes-Benz offered to have their engineers inspect the crash but they were point blank refused access.[155]

It's absolutely logical to speculate that the reason Mercedes' engineers were prevented from inspecting the car is because their precise knowledge of the vehicle

---

[154] *Daily Mail*, "Questions that won't go away," October 21, 2003: http://www.theinsider.org/news/article.asp?id=424
[155] King & Beveridge, *Princess Diana: The Hidden Evidence*; Everard & Houston, *Lady Die: The Diana Conspiracies*: http://www.youtube.com/watch?v=Nr54FXg7ASI

would have allowed them to identify any modifications that had been done on the vehicle. That was precisely what took place after The Boston Brakes assassination of Sir Peter Horsley. We know—direct from no less than SAS veteran Sir Ranulph Fiennes—that the team in control of the assassination made sure that their people restricted access to the vehicle following that "accident" also.[156]

DODI HAD PURCHASED AN ENGAGEMENT RING

Dodi Al-Fayed purchased an engagement ring for Diana and was very clearly about to propose marriage to her—if hadn't done so already. There's no doubt about that. It happened. He bought the ring. There's security footage of him buying it. And the jeweler who sold it to him, Alberto Repossi, has made it crystal clear that he knew that it was an engagement ring for Princess Diana.

But wait, it gets better: Mr. Repossi said that he was pressured by investigators from the official British investigation to change his story and say that it was *not* an engagement ring. He was "intimidated" by Scotland Yard detectives to lie about the ring.

Isn't that interesting? Shouldn't we be the least little bit curious why investigators who are supposed to be looking for the truth would go out of their way to

---

[156] Ibid.

intimidate a responsible witness into telling what they know to be a lie?

DIANA'S BODY WAS ILLEGALLY EMBALMED

Why would you embalm a body when you knew that an autopsy was going to be performed? Well, because you were instructed to, apparently.

Author Jon King summed this point up very well on *The Belzer Connection*:

"There's the question of whether Diana was pregnant. And there's the huge question of why Diana's body was embalmed before it was autopsied. This is against the law in France. It should never have happened. But what it means, rather conveniently, is that it makes null and void any pregnancy test."[157]

The embalming was reportedly "carried out on the orders of a very high-ranking British 'diplomat' who was stationed at the British embassy in Paris on the night of the crash."[158]

DIANA'S PERSONAL PAPERS WERE DESTROYED

---

[157] *The Belzer Connection*, "Lady Di" (dvd), 2003, Jon King.
[158] Richard Coleman, "New Evidence Diana Was Murdered By MI6," citing King & Beveridge, *Princess Diana: The Hidden Evidence*: http://www.consciousape.com/2012/08/21/new-evidence-diana-was-murdered-by-mi6/

It gets even better. While Diana's illegally embalmed body was being returned from France, her stepmother and sister were busy shredding all of Diana's letters. Among things that were known to be in Diana's possession at the time of her death was a box containing audio recordings that she made. Diana had tape-recorded an interview with a valet of Prince Charles, George Smith, who made confidential charges that he had been plied with liquor and brutally raped while in the service of Prince Charles.[159]

On a side note, Diana apparently told him:

"You will get over this. I've been through worse."[160]

Quite sadly, that gives us some idea of what torments Diana may have been going through within the cloaked horrors of the Royal Family.

After her death, Diana's butler helped in a frantic search for those recordings. Her butler knew that Diana had hid the tapes in a wooden box. But the contents of that box disappeared and have never been found. That's a crucial point, because the box, which included other highly sensitive items in addition to the taped interview, was known as Diana's "Crown Jewels" and was regarded as Diana's "insurance policy" against the

---

[159] King & Beveridge, *Princess Diana: The Hidden Evidence*; Everard & Houston, *Lady Die: The Diana Conspiracies*: http://www.youtube.com/watch?v=IJlu08TIT9E
[160] Ibid.

Royals. The Royal Family apparently "secured" its contents immediately after Diana's death.[161]

Diana's loyal butler, Paul Burrell, had been quite disgusted to see Lady Diana's letters and personal belongings destroyed by the Royal Family. He placed some items that he had salvaged—mostly personal things given him by Diana herself—in his home for safekeeping. He was harassed from that moment on for his perceived betrayal of the Royals. The Queen ordered that he should be arrested. His shop was firebombed, his home was searched and he was arrested by police.[162]

In a personal audience with the Queen in December 1997—at the request of Mr. Burrell as a result of his alarm at how Lady Diana's papers and letters were being callously destroyed—the Queen personally warned him. Mr. Burrell said the warning was so stark that, afterward, he feared for the lives of himself and his family. He said the Queen was "deadly serious" looking him straight in the eye and said:

"There are powers at work in this country about which we have no knowledge. Be careful, Paul. No one has been as close to a member of my family as you have."[163]

---

[161] Richard Kay, "Moment of Madness that could destroy Charles, November 2003, *Daily Mail*:
http://www.dailymail.co.uk/debate/columnists/article-228751/Moment-madness-destroy-Charles.html

[162] http://www.youtube.com/watch?v=IJlu08TIT9E

[163] Steve Bird & Sam Lister, "The Queen 'warned butler to beware of dark forces at work'," 11-6-2002, *The Times*:
http://www.thetimes.co.uk/tto/news/uk/article1953372.ece

The warning was meant to be dramatic and was taken that way:

"The Queen warned him that there were dark forces at work in Britain that could threaten him."[164]

BRITISH INTELLIGENCE OFFICIALS WERE IN PARIS

It's also interesting to observe that, at just such an auspicious time, high-ranking members of the intelligence community were right there in Paris at the time of the crash.

Three senior MI6 agents arrived in Paris the day before the accident. Russian intelligence agents in Paris recorded their arrival and were suspicious about the sudden arrival of such a senior group from MI6.[165]

One of those senior MI6 people, Richard Spearman, was an extremely senior MI6 agent, formerly Chief of Staff to the Head of MI6. Mr. Spearman and other MI6 officials were present at the British Embassy in Paris at the time of Diana's death.[166]

According to other sources, including *Executive Intelligence Review*, the incoming Head of MI6, Richard

---

164 Ibid.

165 Reid, "Diana, that SAS murder claim and why it may not be as mad as you think," citing Gennady Sokolov; King & Beveridge, *Princess Diana: The Hidden Evidence*; Everard & Houston, *Lady Die: The Diana Conspiracies*

166 Richard John Charles Tomlinson, "Affidavit of Richard John Charles Tomlinson RE: MI6 and the Princess of Wales," 5-12-1999: http://www.whale.to/b/tomlinson.html

Billing Dearlove, was in Paris in the period prior to the crash of Diana.[167]

Even more disturbing is the report that one of two senior British officials, one of whom was Lord Fellowes, the Private Secretary to Her Majesty The Queen, went into the special communications room of the British Embassy in Paris and—at a very crucial moment—told everyone to clear out of the room, which they did. He commandeered the room for some type of emergency which he neglected to explain. According to one of the operators who was told to leave, that bizarre act occurred at the time when Diana and Dodi were still at the Ritz, preparing to leave. The Queen's Private Secretary, Robert Fellowes, who was also Diana's brother-in-law, was in the French capital an hour before the crash and was seen in the telecommunications room of the British Embassy.[168]

SEALED RECORDS

And oh, by the way:

MI6, roughly the British equivalent to the CIA, has a 400-page dossier on the death of Diana but we won't be seeing it any time soon. The British Government has

---

[167] *Executive Intelligence Review*, "The 'MI6 Factor' in the murder of Princess Diana, 5-14-1999: http://militaryintelligence.mi6govuk.com/2007/12/30/sis_cia_fbi_white_house_pentagon_centcom.aspx

[168] King & Beveridge, *Princess Diana: The Hidden Evidence*; Everard & Houston, *Lady Die: The Diana Conspiracies*: http://www.youtube.com/watch?v=1b4usGUhAOc

placed a 100-year ban on the publication of that document.[169]

CONCLUSIONS

Diana was allowed to bleed to death from very survivable wounds. No other conclusion is medically competent.

"Diana bled to death from the same kind of injuries that President Ronald Reagan survived, because she was never brought to the emergency room operating table until it was too late."

It was *known* that she exhibited the external signs of internal bleeding. It's standard protocol that the only treatment for internal bleeding is surgery at a hospital. Any semblance of decent medical care would have had her at a trauma center in *less than 30 minutes*. This is *Paris* that we're talking about; this is *Princess Diana*. Vast resources were at their immediate disposal. There were Medevac helicopters for emergency transport; high-tech trauma centers a minute away. The fact that she exhibited the external signs of internal bleeding and wasn't at one of those trauma centers within fifteen minutes is inexcusable. And had she been to a hospital within the first hour, she would have survived. But she bled to death, unnecessarily.

---

[169] Everard & Houston, *Lady Die: The Diana Conspiracies*: http://www.youtube.com/watch?v=KSnaki4WKpw

The fact that it took them 1 hour, 40 minutes to get her to where she obviously needed to be reads more like a science fiction from a parallel universe—it's insane! As trained physicians have noted:

"It is absolutely ridiculous that anybody would be sitting there, losing blood—and she was lucent initially—for almost two hours. Because there's protocol for this…and for the French government to come back and say we couldn't even move her because her blood pressure was so low—*ridiculous*!"[170]

As far as the cover story that the driver was drunk and recklessly avoiding the paparazzi, no one has said it better than the father of one of the victims and a friend of Diana, billionaire Mohamed Al-Fayed:

"All bullshit."[171]

I've met Mohamed Al-Fayed. He has world-class security. This isn't the Little Leagues that we're talking about. This is a guy who, when he decides to make some investments, he goes out and buys the Ritz in Paris and Harrods in London. He started from nothing and he didn't get where he is by doing things half-assed. If you think he's going to let his son—who is getting engaged to a famous Princess—get into a car with a driver who is plastered on Prozac and booze, then you have never met Mohamed Al-Fayed. His son had just bought an engagement ring at 6:00 pm that same night. Mohamed is a man who knows how the world works

---

[170] *The Belzer Connection*, "Lady Di" (dvd), 2003, Reika Jakamar.
[171] *The Belzer Connection*, "Lady Di" (dvd), 2003, Mohamed Al-Fayed.

and he knew the whole world would be watching the forthcoming events.

His security team's research learned that the driver's blood sample was changed with one from another of the fifteen bodies present on the same night with Henri Paul, some of whom had committed suicide, with high levels of alcohol and carbon monoxide. *That scenario* actually explains the anomalies. The official version doesn't.

Mohamed also confirmed that Diana had been threatened by the Royal Family:

"Diana was with me for nearly a couple of weeks in Saint Tropez. I knew she was being hassled by Prince Phillip (husband of the Queen). She had already been threatened. And I know, exactly, she was living in danger."[172]

It bears noting that any time that a victim correctly predicts their manner of impending murder, it's a huge red flag. That's the case here. Diana predicted it precisely. And let's speak plainly—this was not a general malaise type of warning. It was a highly specific prediction of the exact way which she thought she would be murdered. And she was.

In the evidence section we covered the anomalies of the case in detail. Now let's lay them out one atop the other and see how they stack up.

---

172 *The Belzer Connection*, "Lady Di" (dvd), 2003, Mohamed Al-Fayed.

CRASH DYNAMICS

The apparent series of events, in order, were as follows:

A. The Mercedes was diverted into the tunnel—which was *not* the way to Dodi's apartment and *not* the intended route—by vehicles intentionally blocking the last exit before the tunnel, which *was* the intended route. This blocking of the exit was seen by eyewitnesses;

B. At least two motorcycles—one with two riders atop it—and one other vehicle ahead of the Mercedes were involved in slowing, blocking and altering of the Mercedes' path as it entered the tunnel. Numerous eyewitness reports substantiate it;

C. A high-intensity strobe light or directed energy weapon was used on the car. It's not completely clear if the purpose was to blind the driver or was a component in the process of commandeering the vehicle's computer system, but *it is very clear* that a high-intensity light was emitted near the entrance to the tunnel, that it played a role in the crash of the Mercedes and that it was *not* simply a camera flash. Numerous eyewitnesses were amazed at the intensity of the light emitted;

D. After the flash of light and near the time of the explosion, the Mercedes "went dark" before it crashed, also according to eyewitness. That feature and the fact that there was an explosion after the flash of light are all factors which are consistent with a high-tech computer hack of the car's electronics system;

E. The loss of control and the crash itself was also consistent with a car hack;

F. The fact that the same Mercedes was stolen at gunpoint a short time prior to the accident and that its computer navigation chip was replaced is another strong indication that the assassination technique used was the computer car hack known colloquially as "The Boston Brakes."[173]

A cover-up quickly ensued, labeling the "accident" as the result of a drunk driver who was recklessly avoiding the pursuing paparazzi. The only problem is that neither of those premises was true: as we established, the photographers' vehicles were nowhere close to the Mercedes and Henri Paul was not drunk. But *hey*—don't let the facts get in the way of a good story.

As Jeffrey Steinberg of *Executive Intelligence Review* observed:

The death of Lady Diana "was unquestionably one of the most significant events to have occurred since the assassination of President John F. Kennedy."

And it bears some striking similarities: Today, all of the essential questions remain unanswered.

- Where is the white Fiat and who was the driver?

---

173 *Princess Diana: The Hidden Evidence*, Jon King & John Beveridge (S.P.I. Books: 2001): http://www.whale.to/c/princess_diana9.html

- What about the lethal level of carbon monoxide found in Henri Paul's blood sample?
- Why did it take the French emergency rescue crew nearly 2 hours to get Diana to the hospital that was less than 4 miles away?[174]

Dignitary protection expert Vince Palamara makes another important observation:

Although there was a public relations campaign to make it appear that Diana walked around unprotected, that is simply not the case. Her security team—especially at the time of her death when she was being protected by elite bodyguards on the payroll of billionaire Mohammed Al-Fayed—was top notch and highly professional. It's often forgotten that one member of that security team actually gave his life while in the service of protecting Diana, and another suffered horrific injuries in the line of duty during the crash.

This tendency to "blame the victim" is one we famously saw in the case of the death of President John F Kennedy, where even some of his own bodyguards—the Secret Service—tried to put the onus on the dead president for the failure in security.[175]

The sudden death of Diana "Queen of Hearts" may have moved the world, but it sure didn't move the Royal Family all that much. The Queen refused to have

---

[174] *The Belzer Connection*, "Lady Di" (dvd), 2003, Jeffrey Steinberg.

[175] Vince Palamara, email to author, October 12, 2013.

the flag flown at half-mast in her honor; *and* refused the request to give her an official State Funeral. They even refused to allow Diana's two sons to go to their mother in Paris. Instead, the boys were forced to follow the mundane Royal Family protocol of going to church that Sunday at Balmoral; at which—incredibly—*no* prayers were said for their mother during the church service. It was clear that the Queen made no effort to change the normal church service to include any mention of Diana.[176]

It was only at Prince Charles' stubborn last-minute insistence that Diana's body was brought back and laid to rest with some appropriate pomp and circumstance. Otherwise, as was noted by the astute British film director, Chris Everard:

"Amazingly, it seems that the Queen would have seen Diana just put into some co-op funeral parlor."[177]

As the British would say: Now isn't that *just lovely*?

In the immediate wake of her death, throngs of British citizens instinctively took to the streets—over *five million* of them, in fact—in an ongoing vigil for their Lady Di. But the media were reportedly instructed not to interview anyone mentioning "murder" even though it was apparently uppermost in many of their minds.[178]

It's important to note that the emotional swell of that crowd was not simply one of sorrow; it was also one of

---

[176] Everard & Houston, *Lady Die: The Diana Conspiracies*: http://www.youtube.com/watch?v=WW-zUfUUwx8
[177] Ibid.
[178] Everard & Houston, *Lady Die: The Diana Conspiracies*: http://www.youtube.com/watch?v=IJlu08TIT9E

anger, and anger that was specifically directed at the Royal Family. Here's an example of one of the many signs that were hung in the streets that evening:

"They Have Your Blood On Their Hands"[179]

I'd say that's pretty direct, wouldn't you? I bet you haven't seen *that* one on your local news!

In fact, we should give a tip of the hat to the British public for their quick suspicions in that regard:

"Make no mistake. It took about ten years for people to realize that President Kennedy had been murdered (by a conspiracy). It took people less than ten *minutes*—certainly no longer than ten hours—to put two and two together and realize that this crash had deliberately been planned and Diana had been assassinated in a form of vehicular homicide. And the crowd knew this and that was the overriding topic. And none of the media reported that properly."[180]

No surprise there, folks.

Prince Philip, husband of the Queen of England, is the man that Mohamed Al-Fayed holds responsible for ordering the death of his son, Dodi, his son's fiancée, Lady Diana, and his security chief at the Paris Ritz Hotel, Henri Paul.

And in case you're wondering whether a member of the Royal Family would actually be capable of such an act, get a load of this. Here are the thoughts of the greatly

---

[179] Ibid.
[180] Ibid.

esteemed His Royal Highness Prince Philip, in his very own words:

"In the event that I am reincarnated, I would like to return as a deadly virus, in order to contribute something to solve overpopulation."[181]

Isn't that sweet? What a nice guy. Of course, in the opinion of some people, Prince Philip doesn't need to come *back* as a virus. He already is one.

It seems that our dear Royal Prince Philip has repeatedly espoused an agenda to reduce the world's population by eighty percent—giving him the dubious distinction of making Adolph Hitler's goals look like child's play by comparison.[182] Members of the world's elite, like—oh, let's just take a wild guess—the Royal Family—are, of course, to be included in the remaining population once it has been "culled" down to get the planet at a "manageable" level.[183] Hence, the purpose of the Prince's desire to come back to us as a virus. *Again.*

No wonder Lady Diana felt like she had to get away from these people. And no wonder that she feared that they'd kill her.

---

[181] *Prison Planet*, "Prince Philip, In His Own Words: We Need To 'Cull' The Surplus Population," 6-10-2004: http://www.prisonplanet.com/Pages/100604_prince_philip.html
[182] *Follow The Money*, "London School of Economics: Reduction of world population by between three to five billion between now and 2050," 12-13-2009: http://seeker401.wordpress.com/2009/12/16/london-school-of-economics-reduction-of-world-population-by-between-three-to-five-billion-people-between-now-and-2050/
[183] *Prison Planet*, "Prince Philip, In His Own Words"

A third witness has corroborated claims from a former SAS sniper (British Special Air Services is the equivalent to U.S. Military Special Operations Command) who boasted that the elite regiment was involved in the deaths of Diana and Dodi Al-Fayed in the Paris tunnel. That has led to efforts in October 2013, by attorneys representing Mohamed Al-Fayed, to reopen the investigation.[184]

As a final word, from all the evidence and witness testimony we've examined, all the indications are that the chart on the following page actually is the way that it happened.

---

[184] John Twomey, "Diana: Time for police to make arrests and seize documents, says lawyer," October 12, 2013, *Daily Express UK*: http://www.express.co.uk/news/royal/436169/Diana-Time-for-police-to-make-arrests-and-seize-documents-says-lawyer

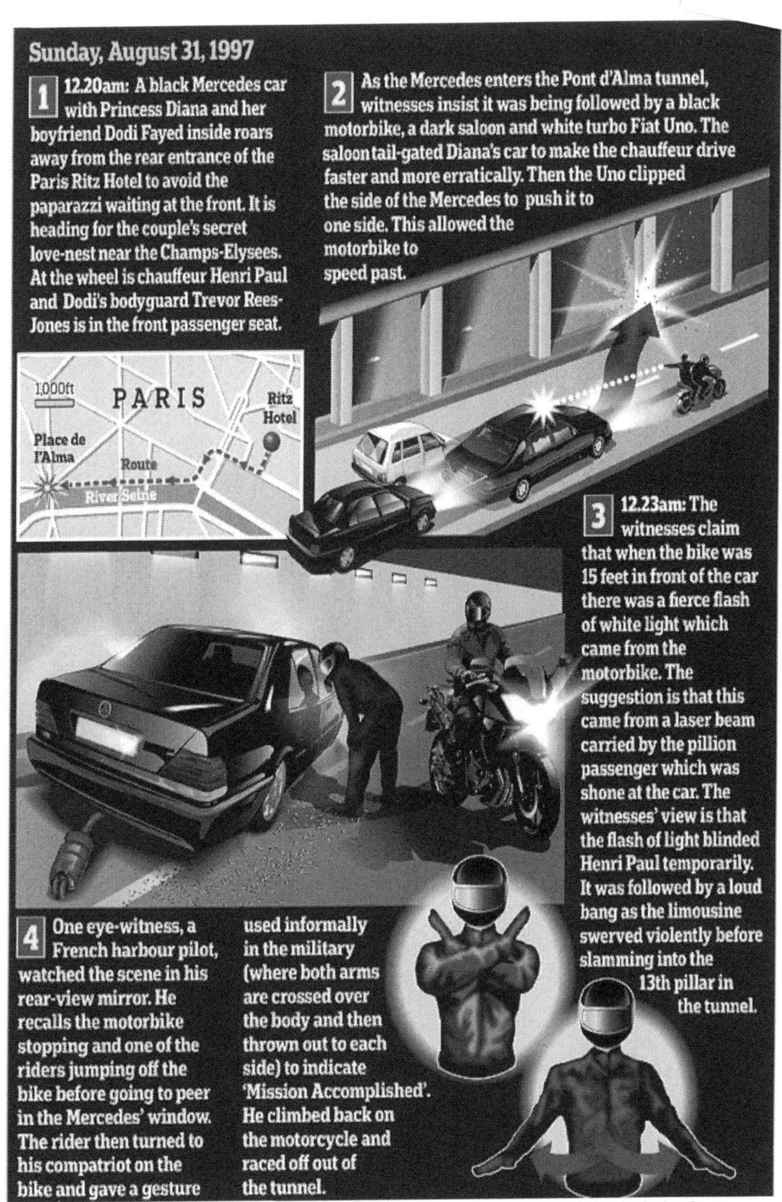

(Chart courtesy of *Daily Mail UK*, August 30, 2013, in Sue Reid: "Diana, that SAS murder claim")

Printed in Great Britain
by Amazon.co.uk, Ltd.,
Marston Gate.